Or Now Is Fine

Choosing to Obey God's Stop! Wait! Go!

Judith Edwards and Perry Edwards

CROSSBOOKS
PUBLISHING

CrossBooks™
A Division of LifeWay
1663 Liberty Drive
Bloomington, IN 47403
www.crossbooks.com
Phone: 1-866-879-0502

First published by CrossBooks 9/17/2010

ISBN: 978-1-6150-7299-6 (sc)

Library of Congress Control Number: 2010911542

Printed in the United States of America

This book is printed on acid-free paper.

Special thanks and gratitude go to Perry's wife Kelley. Her insight and comments added much to our project. Perry and I lived "in the forest" so long that we could only see individual trees; Kelley helped us see the big picture. I called her *friend* before she and Perry married; it has been a joy to watch them build their lives together. Often I have been blessed as I watched them chose to "Obey God's Stop! Wait! Go!"

Judith Edwards

Table of Themes

Moving day! Although hectic, I've always enjoyed the excitement, changes, challenges and activity it brings. While my husband Dalton disconnected the washer, dryer and stove and disassembled the beds, my friend Doris and I packed dishes in the kitchen. Meanwhile our son Perry, who had just come home after his first year of college, and Doris's husband Don were loading items as they became available onto the U-Haul truck. The next item up was a heavy trunk. After surveying the partially filled truck Perry and Don had good news and bad news. They found the perfect spot for the trunk—good news. However, in order to get the trunk to that spot they would have to lift it up and over other furniture and boxes.

Time for a game plan. They each took hold of a side handle as Perry said, "Okay, let's lift it up on *three*. One…" Just as he spoke the word Don heaved the trunk into the air and of course Perry followed suit. The trunk fell into place with a *thud* and the two movers stood back to admire their work. Perry looked at Don and said, "Or Now Is Fine."

That was many years and many moves ago, but I have kept the expression "Or Now Is Fine" alive in the Edwards family. When I need help carrying in the groceries, when I've sat 20 minutes in the pharmacy drive-through, when I'm on hold or impatiently waiting for someone to return a phone call, when five minutes of commercials interrupts a television show I want to watch–I think you get the picture, and that you've been there too. Or Now Is Fine.

More recently my administrative assistant and I were discussing a past-due account. We had been promised payment several times. The latest response was, "We'll pay you soon."

When she told me this I remarked, "Or Now Is Fine!" Then I added, "Hey, you know, that would be a good title for a book!"

Of course I shared my idea with Perry who exclaimed, "I'd like to write it with you! We should do that someday." Then we looked at one another and smiled. "Or Now Is Fine!"

Moving day! You'd think by now we would be experts—but, alas! The plan was to load the heavy stuff first, placing lighter things on top, and working from the front of the truck towards the back. See? Experts! Now for the "alas" part.

No matter how often you move, or how much you plan, it happens every time. If we were building a house, it would be like trying to fit a basement in *after* the foundation slab has been poured, the walls raised, roof in place, and shingles nailed down.

If we were making an ice cream dessert, it would be like trying to place the brownie in the dish *after* you already had two scoops of ice cream, hot fudge, crushed nuts, sprinkles, and the cherry, held by the stem, poised to be placed on top.

If we were loading a U-Haul truck, it would be like—hey, wait! We *were* loading a U-Haul truck. And it was *after* we had already loaded all of the heavy stuff, topped it off with some lighter boxes, and even placed some of the fragile things on top. That's when we were told that there was one more "thing" out in the office. The "thing" was a trunk. A footlocker-style trunk. A heavy-looking-Army-issue-footlocker-style trunk. But who were we to judge the weight of the trunk by its looks?

Ever heard of first impressions? Well—our initial assessment of the trunk was correct. It *was* heavy.

So here we stand, at the back of the U-Haul, trying to figure out how we will get this heavy-looking-Army-issue-steel-reinforced-brass-trimmed-footlocker-style trunk to fit somewhere in the middle of what we have already done. If you haven't noticed by now that it had been a long day and our energy was spent, I'd be glad to describe that trunk again!

We did find a great place; the only problem was that we would have to lift the item up over some of the lighter things, with me balancing one foot on a recliner and the other wedged between some boxes marked "breakables." Knowing we would have to work together to "heave" it into place I said to Don, "Okay, let's lift it up on three. One..."

He yanked his end of the trunk up off the bed of the truck and shoved it forward! The only thing between that trunk and its resting spot was ME! I leaned backwards, threw my side of the trunk up too, twisted my body out of the way, and–*perfect fit!*

It was a wonderful fit! BUT HE NEARLY TOOK OFF MY HEAD!!

I was frustrated, and relieved, as we stood there looking at the great placement of that trunk. I'm sure it was a text-book passive aggressive statement but I muttered, under my breath but loud enough to be heard, "Or now is fine."

SEND	To.	Perry@Tyler.com
	From. . .	Mom@ABQ.com
	Subject:	Write a book?

Hey, were you serious when you said you'd like for us to write a book together?

SEND	To.	Mom@ABQ.com
	From. . .	Perry@Tyler.com
	Subject:	RE: Write a book?

Are you kidding? That would be GREAT!! And really, really scary! What are you thinking? What would it look like? How would we start? Oh, yeah, these are questions you deal with all the time as a writer and editor, aren't they?

Kelley has been suggesting I write a book for several years. And recently I've been praying about it but didn't know how to do anything about it. So . . . I guess I'm saying, "You bet!"

So–the idea was born, the commitment made and the project begun. Emails, texts and one hour phone conversations. Midnight ideas that seemed great at the time. (What *were* we thinking?) Notes jotted down in church, in doctors' offices and while sitting in ten minute meetings that were squeezed into an hour. Paper clip chains made while staring at the computer screen. What seemed like a good idea in the beginning was becoming a bit more complicated!

As we began to write we made discoveries about ourselves. While we are very much alike, as you have just discovered we also have some very different perspectives and of course writing styles. While I had told the story many times through the years as a funny anecdote, I had not even considered that Perry might not feel just as I did. Nor had I realized that his head was in jeopardy!

We also discovered that the very phrase "Or Now Is Fine" can be interpreted and applied in so many ways. Need a new car? Time to upgrade your laptop and printer? You *could* wait till the sale goes off…Or Now Is Fine! It can be a reminder to "seize the day;" it can be the reality that we are "smack dab in the middle" of a situation where we have no choice but to "throw the trunk." It can be said with enthusiasm, sarcasm, as a question or with resignation and a shrug of the shoulders. It might be interpreted, "Let's get this show on the road," or in John Wayne terminology, "We're burnin' daylight." It's quite possible we find ourselves in a situation where we'd rather not be, but when we hear God say He'll be with us, we can say, "Or Now Is Fine." Whatever the circumstances, tone of voice or attitude, the bottom line is that God is always leading us according to *His* plans—in *His* timing. If we truly live in obedience to Him, we will say "now is fine" when we hear God speaking to us.

S E N D	To.	Perry@Tyler.com
	From. . .	Mom@ABQ.com
	Subiect:	An Idea

I can see lots of possibilities for a book—because, as I've started thinking and writing about it, the idea of "Or Now Is Fine" pretty much touches where we all are living in one way or another. So we have our title and theme, but we need a subtitle that describes to others the direction we are headed. And ideas?

SEND	To.	Mom@ABQ.com
	From. . .	Perry@Tyler.com
	Subject:	RE: An Idea

Kelley came up with a suggestion. What do you think about this: "Choosing to Obey God's Stop! Wait! Go!"? It's the crux of our walk with God. We face those three decisions every day—in our speech, our actions, our decisions—when to step out and move forward, or hold back and watch, or even stop what we are doing altogether. Makes you think of those scriptures like "Be still and know that I am God"/"Stand firm"/"March around the wall seven times." ☺ It fits with the title because hearing God's voice and choosing to act in obedience could mean we do any of those three things at God's leading . . . not ours!

SEND	To.	Perry@Tyler.com
	From. . .	Mom@ABQ.com
	Subject:	Re: An Idea

I think that's great! Thanks, Kelley! Looks like we are thinking on the same page.

So, what format shall we use for the book? Maybe we could make it like a collage of "bits and pieces"—stories, examples from the Bible, devotionals we both write, real life illustrations—a variety of ways to develop the theme. As hospital chaplain, you send weekly "Faith Boosts" to your hospital staff. We would definitely incorporate those. We could divide the book into sections built around themes such as worship, following and obeying Him, waiting on Him . . . you get the idea.

I'm thinking we would put what you write in one font, and mine in another font, so the reader can tell who is "speaking." We might even include some of the emails we wrote to one another while working together on the book!

S E N D	To.	Mom@ABQ.com
	From. . .	Perry@Tyler.com
	Subiect:	RE: An Idea

Sounds like you've already got the plan! That makes it easier. I like the idea about writing in a devotional/bit-and-pieces/stories style. That is pretty much how our "Faith Boosts" are written each week here at the hospital.

    Okay, I've talked with Kelley, we've both prayed about it, and I'm ready to go!

S E N D	To.	Perry@Tyler.com
	From. . .	Mom@ABQ.com
	Subiect:	Re: An Idea

Okay, let's do it! On three . . . Or Now Is Fine!

The military dictator was gleaming. The battle appeared to be successful. The troops were scattered and the Leader was dead. Could it get any better than this? He was at the height of his game.

    The generals stood as he entered the war room. It wasn't so much out of respect. It was more from fear. He was ruthless; they had all felt the sting of his anger and vengeance. He spoke loudly, hoping it would make him sound more authoritative. Could they hear the anxiety? Could they see the beads of sweat? Did his eyes show how nervous he felt? "What is the count? Does anyone here know the count?"

    Who would speak first? The ones with the most tenure? The newest rookies with nothing to lose? Who would it be? It ended up being a young lieutenant who stood, trembling, as he spoke of messages intercepted and plans uncovered. "The first major offensive began as we overran their headquarters and captured their leader. We made an example of him, in public, and his troops fled. We feel sure we have obtained a decisive victory, except for..." His voice squeaked and trailed off.

    "Except for WHAT?!!", the dictator roared.

    "Except for the last message. All we were able to decode was these words: **'When I count to *three*'.**"

At that moment, "There was a violent earthquake, for an angel of the Lord came down from heaven and, going to the tomb, rolled back the stone and sat on it. His appearance was like lightning, and his clothes were white as snow. The guards were so afraid of him that they shook and became like dead men. The angel said to the women, 'Do not be afraid, for I know that you are looking for Jesus, who was crucified. He is not here; He has risen, just as He said'" (Matt. 28:2-6a NIV).

Or now is fine!

The writer of **Ecclesiastes** says that "He has made everything appropriate in its time" (Eccl. 3:11 HCSB). Verses 1-15 capture the heart of what "Or Now Is Fine" is all about.

I am fascinated by both the wealth of contrasts and the realities hidden in Ecclesiastes 3:1–15. For me, these fifteen verses capture the heart of what *Or Now Is Fine* is all about. Listen to the words of the Preacher: "There is an occasion for everything, and a time for every activity under heaven:
a time to give birth and a time to die;
a time to plant and a time to uproot;
a time to kill and a time to heal;
a time to tear down and a time to build;
a time to weep and a time to laugh;
a time to mourn and a time to dance;
a time to throw stones and a time to gather stones;
a time to embrace and a time to avoid embracing;
a time to search and a time to count as lost;
a time to keep and a time to throw away;
a time to tear and a time to sew;
a time to be silent and a time to speak;
a time to love and a time to hate;
a time for war and a time for peace"
(Eccl. 3:1–8 HCSB).
Then the Preacher adds, "He has made everything appropriate in its time" (v. 11). I think you get the picture! Let's consider a few more *Or Now Is Fine* times.

* **Time to obey God's Go!** Picture this: the late-night Western is in full swing. The troops are poised and ready for action. A John Wayne-style commander calls out "Charge!" (Translation: *now is fine!*) The bugle sounds the charge and the troops lunge forward, ready for battle.

God planned to give the city of Jericho to Joshua, but it had to be done just as God said (see Joshua 6). For six days the Israelites were to circle the walls and then, on the seventh day, they would blow their trumpets, the walls would fall down, and they would have the victory. In preparation for this great happening, Joshua gave these instructions: "Don't shout. In fact, don't even speak—not so much as a whisper until you hear me say, 'Shout!'—then shout away!" (Josh. 6:10 TMB). *Now Is Fine to Obey God's "Go!"*

> **?** What if, on the sixth day, the Israelites had said, "We've
> • done this six times and nothing has happened. Maybe we
> should stop"? Have you prepared and planned and done your
> homework? Has the time for action arrived? You know the rest
> of your story. Have you heard the bugler's call to action lately?
> Is it time to charge? Time to obey God's Go!?

The word *now* often carries with it a sense of urgency. On Palm Sunday afternoon in 1994, I stood at my living room window in Alabama trying to take in the beauty surrounding me. To this desert girl from New Mexico, it seemed that the entire state was in full bloom—including the weeds! The sight of the white flowers on more than a dozen dogwood trees was breathtaking.

The weather had been turbulent all day, but my New Mexico mind told me not to be too concerned. Then I turned on the television to watch the five o'clock news; newsman James Spann pointed at an approaching tornado on the radar screen. "If you live in this area," Spann said, "go *now* to your safest place."

My husband, Dalton, had gone to the storm cellar before, but I'd always just gone to the basement. This time Dalton was out of town. James Spann sounded serious, so I decided to take his advice. At 5:32 p.m., the tornado he'd pointed out tore through our Birmingham suburb.

The first thing I saw when I opened the storm cellar door was the root ball of a large hickory tree. With fifteen minutes of daylight left, I hurried to survey the damage. A hundred-year-old oak tree lay atop the house. Windows on three sides were blown out, and the carport balanced precariously on one support post. (I discovered the next morning that the two houses beside ours were totally destroyed, and we had lost about thirty-five of the trees in our yard. The dogwoods I'd admired moments before heading for shelter lay on the ground, covered with mud.)

In the eerie silence, the only sounds were distant wailing sirens, the occasional loud crack of another tree falling, and water from the damaged roof dripping into every upstairs room. I lit some candles, built a fire in the fireplace, and began preparing for what would no doubt be a long night. Then I sat down at the piano and began to play the hymn "How Great Thou Art." "I see the stars (right through my ceiling!). I hear the rolling thunder (literally). My God, how great Thou art."

So often the word *now* carries with it a call to action, a call to make a choice. I had no idea when I decided to go to the cellar what was about to be unleashed right on top of me. However, I've been thankful so many times that I made the right choice.

I pray that when God tells me it's time to **go now** I will choose to move in sync with Him and depend on past lessons, on His wisdom and on the counsel of others. I also pray that I will always be able to see His awesome greatness—even through the holes in the ceiling.

* Time to obey God's Stop! or Retreat. I have a friend who, along with his wife and three young daughters, recently spent five years as missionaries in Brazil. My friend supervised the building of dozens of churches. Thousands came to know the Lord as a result of the family's ministry. They hosted hundreds of mission groups with their daughters (who quickly learned Portuguese) translating.

I just received a letter telling of the family's decision to leave the country they've come to love. My friend wrote, "Please know that this is not an easy decision for us. We have poured so much of ourselves into Brazil that it is hard to imagine living anywhere else." Yet, they heard God's call to change direction.

Another friend I'll call Carla illustrates another aspect of retreating. Carla lived with an abusive husband for almost fifteen years. She prayed for him and, when he refused to go for counseling, she went alone. She did her best to live at peace with him. Finally, fearing for her own and her children's safety, Carla made the difficult decision to leave. It wasn't easy, but it was time to retreat.

? Is it time for you to retreat? Maybe you feel you've taught
• that Sunday school class as long as you should. Is it time for a

younger person to accept some responsibility? Does God have a new assignment for you? Why are you staying in the job you can't stand? List the reasons for staying and for going. If you feel you must stay, how can you change your attitude to make the job better or, at the very least, more bearable? Many difficult decisions can be mountains we don't want to climb. Pray for wisdom. Seek the counsel of trusted, godly friends. Search God's Word for answers. Listen for the bugle. Is it sounding *charge* or *retreat*?

* **Time to just stand still, obeying God's Wait!** "Be still, and know that I am God" (Ps. 46:10 KJV), or as Peterson says in *The Message*, "Step out of the traffic! Take a long, loving look at me, your High God, above politics, above everything" (TMB). I wonder if sometimes God doesn't want to take me firmly by the shoulders and say, "If you'll just *stop* for a minute! Don't move forward; don't put it in reverse. Just *be still*."

? Are God's hands on *your* shoulders? Can you hear Him saying, "Be still so you can listen to Me. Choose your priorities. Stop doing the unimportant. Focus on the essential."?

* **Time to speak.** You sit on the platform trying to listen to the three other speakers. Your instinct is to sneak off the platform and run as fast as you can. What do you have to say that could possibly interest these people? Why in the world did you say *yes* when asked to do this? The moderator steps up to the podium. Your heart skips a beat as you hear her call your name. It's too late to run. *Or Now Is Fine!* Step up, speak up and give it all you've got!

The scenario just described is very different from the rest of life. You rehearse a speech. You may even have notes at hand. But life isn't rehearsed. No one supplies cue cards and Teleprompters for real life. And yet, you may need to speak words of:

Encouragement,
Loving counsel,
Sympathy or empathy,
Laughter,
Interest,
Caution.

The year 2009 began with a *bang* in our household. In less than two weeks' time, my husband Dalton was diagnosed with myelodysplastic syndrome and began a series of forty-two chemotherapy treatments in addition to a number of other treatments and tests. Considering that he had been diagnosed with Parkinson's disease just over a year before, we knew we were destined for a long road ahead. By the time December 31 arrived, my calendar documented 106 medical appointments.

After spending so many hours in the oncology clinic, we became part of the family of infusion nurses, schedulers and lab techs. On our first visit after a three-week break, infusion nurse Regina met me at the door and reached out for a hug.

"I couldn't wait for you to get here," she whispered. "My son killed himself last week."

We might have been unwilling ambassadors, but the truth was that all those times Regina had been injecting a drug called Vidaza into Dalton's veins, God had been infusing her with His love through two of His ambassadors.

? Just a few weeks ago, we received news that a very special friend has been diagnosed with a rare form of multiple myeloma. Today his port was implanted. Because of Dalton's diagnosis, I knew how to relate to his wife. Because of Dalton's diagnosis, we knew the questions to ask and understood our friends' questions and misgivings. Who needs your encouragement today? Can God speak through your experience to help someone else?

"An anxious heart weighs a man down, but a kind word cheers him up." (Prov. 12:25 NIV)

"A word aptly spoken is like apples of gold in settings of silver." (Prov. 25:11 NIV)

My wife's mother had a heart catheter recently. She told us about it over the weekend. Not good timing when telling someone who works in a hospital. It took all that I've got *not* to call any number of my co-workers in our Cardiac program—bright and early Sunday morning. You know, there is that proverb that states, *"If a man loudly blesses his neighbor early in the morning, it will be taken as a curse*" (Prov. 27:14 NIV). My wife didn't want me to be a "curse" to anyone with whom I work.

So I waited. And I waited. And Kelley kept asking me questions that I couldn't answer. And *finally* Monday morning came around and I could *run* into the hospital and ask my questions. Ok, I didn't actually run. You see, God knew my anxious heart and He prepared comfort in the parking lot. I saw "someone" from Cardiac and began asking my questions. As we walked in together, he gave me his attention as if he had all the time in the world—as if there weren't any other patients in the hospital that day. What a gift!

But the greater gift came the next morning. On the day of her cath, this same person hollered across the parking lot (again, a God-given timing thing), "What time?" I just heard a loud voice. I wasn't sure what was yelled or who was yelling. When I turned, there he was, hollering out again. "What time?" I responded that it would be at 9:00 a.m. and he said, "I know what I'll be doing at that time then." Certainly the greater gift—that he remembered and would take time to pray for my mother-in-law – whom he doesn't even know!

Back to our verses in Proverbs. I was definitely cheered up by a golden apple. And the apple was set in silver when my father-in-law called to say she came through her procedure just fine. And my anxious heart was cheered once more as I was given even *more* time to ask *more* questions about what would happen next with stents, balloons, catheter, etc.

We are just one little family going through some bumps in the road on our health journey. There are many, many more that we see each day at East Texas Medical Center where I work. Magnify that by 100's of hospitals around our nation and millions of sick and hurting people around the world. We may not be able to speak to every anxious heart. Our words may not grow like golden apples for everyone. But we can speak grace to each other today. One at a time. Here in this place. In whatever place God has placed you.

Hand an apple of gold to the next person you see. It just might be the "turnover" that person needs.

* * * * *

* **Time to be silent.** Don't you just love those times when you think of something to say, you re-consider, and you remain silent? I'm afraid they come too few and far between for me. I am more like my friend Herb, who says that he likes to hear what he has to say for the first time along with everyone else!

Have you ever thought, "I just don't know what to say?" That might be a pretty good indicator that you are to say nothing! Years ago John

Drakeford wrote a book titled *The Awesome Power of the Listening Ear.* So often the best words spoken are no words at all.

The Healing Sound of Silence

They hated
They plotted
They marched
They accused

They tore at His clothing
His body they bruised

They mocked Him
They nailed Him
Chose thorns
Wove a hood

They screamed out in anger
But silent He stood

He prayed
He wept
He accepted
He healed

His faulty accusers
His Light soon revealed

He hung
He pardoned
He died
On the wood

The earth shook in mourning
Now silent they stood
          (Adapted from the Gospel of Matthew, chapters 26 & 27)

We question

He answers
We search
He is found

His arms wrap around us
Our eyes to the ground

We grieve
We're downhearted
On dark paths
We trod

And softly, He whispers
"Be still. I am God."

Precious Savior, in the fast-paced schedule we've carved out for ourselves today, remind us of our deep need for silence–to be still and remember the powerful work of the cross.

———————————————————

* **Time to stop worrying.** One of my friends says that ninety-five percent of what we worry about never happens; therefore worry is a good idea! "Donald" says his mother-in-law's spiritual gift is worrying. I know, of course, that there is *never* a good time to worry and in my best intentions, I *want* to release my concerns to His care. However, convincing myself of that truth at 1:15 a.m. is sometimes not as simple as it should be. Do you know what I mean?

As Christ followers, we have been given some wonderful gifts–the gifts of love, joy, peace, patience, kindness, goodness, faith, gentleness and self-control (see Gal. 5:22-23). A thief is waiting to rob us of these gifts–the thief of worry. There is no way we can be joyful if worried thoughts clog our minds. Soon all the other gifts are sucked into the worry pool as the thief continues to gain control. Christ's advice is that we not "worry about tomorrow, because tomorrow will worry about itself. Each day has enough trouble of its own" (Matt. 6:34 HCSB).

The story is told of a man driving through the countryside at night. Suddenly he realized he had a flat tire, and sure enough, he had no jack. Seeing a farmhouse in the distance, he began to walk. As he got closer he thought, "I will probably have to climb over a fence to get to the house, and will just about rip my pants." A bit further he thought, "There is probably a bull in the pasture; he will surely charge me." With the house drawing ever closer the man thought, "They probably have a mean dog in the yard and he will attack me." Just before he reached the front gate he thought, "They are probably getting ready for bed, will turn out the lights just as I get there and will be upset because I bothered them."

Finally arriving at the front porch, he stepped up to the door and angrily rang the bell. When the farmer opened the door the traveler shouted, "Just keep your old jack! I didn't want it anyway!"

That wasn't the way Paul said we should live. His advice was, "Do not be anxious about anything, but in everything, by prayer and petition, with thanksgiving, present your requests to God" (Phil. 4:6 NIV). I especially like the way Peterson puts it in *The Message*: "Don't fret or worry. Instead of worrying, pray. Let petitions and praises shape your worries into prayers, letting God know your concerns. Before you know it, a sense of God's wholeness, everything coming together for good, will come and settle you down. It's wonderful what happens when Christ displaces worry at the center of your life" (Phil. 4:6-7 TMB).

> ❓ Shape your worries into prayer! I like that. What worries do
> • you have right now that need to be shaped into prayers? Now
> is a fine time to do that, *choosing* to lay your burdens in His
> arms. He is your Shepherd. You can just assume the role of a
> dumb sheep, secure in the knowledge that the Shepherd will
> not lead you into but rather away from danger. If remembering
> that is still not enough, write your worries on paper. Then edit
> what you have written, changing the words into a prayer. And
> may the "peace of God, which surpasses every thought, guard
> your hearts and minds in Christ Jesus" (Phil. 4:7 HCSB).

* Time to put away unrealistic anticipations. I heard someone say that expectations are premeditated resentments. Think about it. You're sure it's going to be a wonderful Christmas. Everyone will be home; you will build a fire in the fireplace and sing Christmas carols. The meal, the weather and the children's behavior will all be perfect. By the end of the day, with hugs all around, everyone will go home, thankful to have had such a wonderful time. Reality check: the roads are icy so everyone arrives late. The turkey doesn't thaw fast enough; the pumpkin pie boils over and burns in the oven. FM (family member) 1 has a cold and is grouchy; FM 2 and FM 3 argued so their children, FMs 4-6, are also fussing. No one really wants to sing; besides, the guys want to watch a ball game. By the time everyone finally leaves, you look at the dishes yet to be washed and wonder what went wrong. Nothing went *wrong*. You expected perfection; reality happened.

We can become a prisoner to hope. If all our focus is on anticipation of better days, healthier relationships, healed bodies, more money and/ or time, second chances and unrealistic expectations we overlook the opportunities that are ours today.

* **Time to forgive.** Give up resentment. It is like taking poison and hoping the other person dies. When you give someone the gift of forgiveness you in return receive two gifts–those of peace and happiness. Like you, I have seen so many examples of those who allowed an unforgiving spirit to grip them. I sat beside a ninety year old man as he was dying. His final words, with resentment in his voice, were a story about the mistreatment, as a teenager, he received from his father.

When he was fifty-eight "Leon" finally forgave his mother for abandoning him as an infant. "Eddie's" wife embezzled money from the family business to help her unwed, pregnant sister. When the embezzlement was revealed both the wife and her sister begged for forgiveness, but Eddie refused to meet with them. His sense of betrayal was so great he could not cross the wall of bitterness.

My pastor recently preached a series of sermons about Joseph. If anyone had a "right" to hold a grudge, surely Joseph qualified. (You can read his story again in Genesis 37-50.) Yet when his first son was born Joseph named him Manasseh, "God has made me forget all my hardship in my father's house" (Gen. 41:51 HCSB). He made the choice to let go of and move beyond past hurts. Then as the drama unfolds we find Joseph's life painting a beautiful picture of forgiveness. Because his eyes were set on God's timetable, God's "Stop! Wait! Go!" and not on the wrongs done to him in the past, Joseph became our role model for a forgiving spirit.

Paul's advice was to forget what is behind us and reach forward to what lies ahead (see Phil. 3:13). Only with a forgiving spirit can we do that. Jesus was very specific about our need to forgive; He was also very generous in forgiving us. Not only does an unforgiving spirit bind us; it makes a mockery of the forgiveness we have been given.

? Is there someone you need to forgive? Remember, forgiveness
is a choice. Take a piece of paper and write these words:
"_____, *I forgive you.*" It won't be instantaneous, and
no, you won't forget the wrong. But you will have loosened
one of the links of the chain that binds you. Are you the one
who needs to ask for forgiveness?

Perhaps *you* are the person you need to forgive. Now is a good time to
discover anew the blessed gift of God's love, forgiveness and grace. I heard
the testimony of a woman who, as a teenager, had lived a very tumultuous
life. She wanted to release her burdens to the Lord but could not believe
that He could really forgive the terrible things she had done.

After a lengthy discussion, her pastor saw that he was getting nowhere.
He reached for his Bible, opened it to 1 John 1:9, and began reading, "If
we confess our sins, he is faithful and just to forgive us our sins, all except
having an abortion and using drugs."

Shocked, the young woman said, "*That's* not what it says."

"Exactly," replied the pastor. In a flood of tears the young woman
confessed her sins, started on the road to self-forgiveness, and accepted
Christ's "cleansing from all unrighteousness."

Remember the *Where's Waldo* books? The goal is to find a certain man, Waldo,
in a busy picture full of people. Waldo dresses in a red and white striped shirt
and shellfish hat, carries a wooden walking stick, and wears glasses. He is always
losing things, including books, camping equipment and even his shoes, and
readers are invited to spot these items in the illustrations as well.

Let's do the same thing with part of the Gospel of Luke. In the 5th chapter
there is a story about Jesus, a crowd, some Pharisees and teachers, a paralyzed
man, and some friends. And here's the question: "Where's (insert YOUR name)?"
Take a look at this story and put yourself into the picture, choosing a different
place for you each time.

See yourself as one of the crowd. Are you close to Jesus? Far away in a
distant corner of the room? Are you bored? Excited? Too hot from the closeness
of the others in the crowd? Can you hear? Are you distracted by the falling
ceiling tiles or intimidated by the religious leaders?

See yourself as a Pharisee. Are you there because you're curious? Do you
want to hide that curiosity from the other Pharisees? Is something religious

happening? Are you cynical? Are you putting-on-airs to impress the commoners around you? Do you want to believe but you're scared?

See yourself as a friend of the paralyzed man. Are you hopeful? Are you frustrated with the crowds? Is he heavy? Did you have other plans today? Is he really a friend—and would he count you as one? Was it your idea to tear up someone else's house? Did you try to stop the others from damaging this roof? Do you want to hide your face?

I can see me in the faces of each of these groups. I'm proud of my faith in some pictures, embarrassed by my pride in others. But I've never seen me as the paralyzed man. After all, *I'm not paralyzed!* Or am I?

Now I see it! There I am! Oh, what a terrible picture of pain and suffering. Paralyzed with fear—so that I can't walk over to that hurting person to offer comfort. Paralyzed with pride—so that I think I'm above so many things and so many people. Paralyzed with sin—so that I can't walk in the way of the Messiah.

But like it or not, there I am, paralyzed and weighed down by all the burdens and trauma in life, looking up into the eyes of Jesus. And He is looking straight at me…finding ME in the crowd of faces. And He says, "*Friend,* your sins are forgiven." **Ultimate healing!** And as if that isn't enough…more than my heart and mind can take in or understand…He then says, "I tell you, get up, take your mat and go home." Or, roughly translated: "You are not paralyzed by spiritual death or physical inability anymore!"

Where's Waldo books are fun if you're interested in searching for a "face in the crowd."

He was interested in a search too. And He found your face.

---

* **Time to Pray.** When is the right time to pray? I wonder if we don't sometimes forget that *now* is the time—now meaning those all-of-a-sudden, spontaneous moments that happen throughout the day, reminding us that we have a Father Who wants to hear from us. Do your children need a special occasion to talk with you? Sometimes—but hopefully not all the time.

Paul certainly wanted his readers to understand the importance of a continual prayer/conversation relationship with our Teacher. To his caution not to worry he added, "but in *everything*, through *prayer and petition* with *thanksgiving*, let your *requests* be made known to God." Then once again we are reminded of that precious promise—that as we pray "the peace of God, which surpasses all comprehension, will guard your hearts and your minds in Christ Jesus" (Phil. 4:6-7 NASB).

Even if we are not specifically, consciously involved in a prayer conversation, Paul next tells us how to direct our thoughts so that we can better focus on and be ready for spontaneous prayer. "Whatever is true, whatever is honorable, whatever is just, whatever is pure, whatever is lovely, whatever is commendable—if there is any moral excellence and if there is any praise—dwell on these things" (Phil 4:6-8 HCSB). Or as Peterson says in *The Message,* "filling your minds and meditating on things true, noble, reputable, authentic, compelling, gracious—the best, not the worst; the beautiful, not the ugly; things to praise, not things to curse." That sounds pretty much like prayer to me; what do you think?

Can you just imagine what Paul would have accomplished had he owned a BlackBerry, iPod, PDA, or even a cell phone while in his prison cell? Our choices of communication channels today border on unbelievable, don't they? Just when I think I finally acquired the newest, most innovative option something even more astonishing appears on the shelf, intimidating my "perfect" device. My first computer operated on a single floppy disc; then I moved up in the world. I got a *dual floppy!* I remember thinking, after hearing about computers with hard drives, that I would *never* need that much memory on a computer!

But you are already way ahead of me, aren't you? Our communication channels with God reach way beyond Wi-Fi capabilities, are faster than the highest speed network, and we never have to be worried about a *fatal error.* The only "viruses" that can damage our communication channels are those we allow to infiltrate, and confession, repentance and renewal of our minds are the best anti-virus programs available.

Remember that wonderful feeling of opening the mailbox and finding a letter addressed to you? You want to read it as soon as possible...ripping the envelope apart as you stand in the driveway. You rush through it the first time—you savor it the second, third, etc.

Times have changed but the joy is the same. Now we e-mail or text each other. Maybe our connection is on Face Book or MySpace. Whatever the method, our soul is blessed.

Imagine what it felt like to receive a letter from the Apostle Paul. One of the Elders would stand up in front of the group of worshippers and pull out the message. Folks were eager to hear what he has to say, soaking up every word, not wanting to miss *anything*! And then he gives them a SECOND gift—as if receiving the letter itself wasn't enough!

"God, whom I serve with my whole heart in preaching the gospel of his Son, is my witness how constantly I remember you in my prayers at all times" (Rom. 1:9 NIV).

"I always thank God for you" (I Cor. 1:4 NIV).

"I thank my God every time I remember you. In all my prayers for all of you, I always pray with joy" (Phil. 1:4 NIV).

"We always thank God, the Father of our Lord Jesus Christ, when we pray for you " (Col. 1:3 NIV).

"We always thank God for all of you, mentioning you in our prayers" (I Thess. 1:2 NIV).

"We ought always to thank God for you, brothers, and rightly so" (2 Thess. 1:3 NIV).

"… night and day I constantly remember you in my prayers" (2 Tim. 1:3 NIV).

A song from a few years back talked about the same thing.

"Somebody's praying, I can feel it. Somebody's praying for me.
Mighty hands are guiding me to protect me from what I can't
see. Somebody's praying for me."

Several years ago I discovered the ministry of prayer walking— "praying on sight with insight." My first international prayer walk venture was in Zimbabwe. Some of our mission workers were unable to secure work visas, so a small group of us walked around the government buildings in downtown Harare, that country's capital city. Unable to pray aloud, we none-the-less spoke with our Lord as we walked. Less than a month after we arrived back in the States we received word: without explanation, the visas had been approved.

The day before we were to leave the country our leader drove us to a point where we could turn 360 degrees and look at that city, home of so much lost-ness and suffering. On our way out that morning we drove past a line of men that extended just over four blocks. When I asked what they were doing, I was told that they were day laborers, hoping to have work just for that day. A couple of hours later, as we began praying from our high vantage point, our leader suggested that we use the Lord's Prayer as our model. When my mouth voiced the words, "Give us this day our daily bread," you can imagine the picture that came to my mind. God taught me so many lessons that day. I gained a new empathy for the millions of hungry people who had previously just been faces. I glimpsed the compassionate heart of those who have committed their lives to share the Bread of Life with the spiritually hungry. And I learned to say with new appreciation, "Thank You for the bread I have experienced—the wheat bread and the Bread that symbolizes the Body broken for me."

Since that first experience I have prayerwalked in many other places...a remote fishing village in Maranhao, Brazil; on the streets of Bangkok, Thailand, home to some 12 million people; on the London subway and ski resorts in Canada. But perhaps the most amazing discovery has been that I can prayerwalk in the mall and in the oncology clinic; I can prayer ride on an airplane and pray around the world as I watch the evening news. I can prayerwalk the auditorium as fellow worshipers gather on Sunday morning and I can prayerwalk the conference room where I will soon be speaking. I can prayer drive through dangerous parts of town, and I can prayer sing on 35th Circle as I walk my Shih Tzu, Miss Lottie Moon.

The right time to pray? Oh, yes, *now* is definitely fine. You don't *have to wait* till you count to three! Prayer is not an appointed time, a ritual, duty or habit; prayer is a lifestyle of communication and fellowship with God.

I felt that old, familiar twinge again this morning...the one that reminds me that I am "fearfully and wonderfully made." The doctor said it was a ruptured disc but God has made it obvious, over and over again, that it is just a reminder of Who He is and what He is doing in my life. Confused? Let me fill you in.

You see, I've had two surgeries on my back to fix discs that just didn't want to grow old with me. The first one "exploded" (not my word—I'm just going on the doctor's story here) so suddenly that the vertebra rubbed together and splintered off fragments of bone into my spinal column. No big deal. I thought surgery fixed *everything* at that time in my life and so I jumped at it. It did stop the pain for several years but I didn't see God in it. So He got my attention again. A second disc decided to join the first.

That second one ruptured so completely that there wasn't any disc material left to provide any type of cushion. (Again, I'm going on the doctor's story.) So the doctor put in a "surgical cushion" to provide what had been lost with that disc. I have no idea what it is or what he was talking about. I just know I can bend, twist, move, and have some sense of mobility that I would have lost if they had fused those bones in my back. And **that** is where God woke me up to what He is doing.

Ezekiel 22:30 says, *"I (God talking) looked for a man among them who would build up the wall and stand before Me in the gap on behalf of the land so I would not have to destroy it, but I found none"* (NIV).

23

I have a cushion that is "standing in the gap" for me so that I am able to move in just about any way I choose. God is calling for folks who will "stand in the gap" so the Spirit can move among people. Does He have to use us? No. Does He <u>choose</u> to use us? Yes. And that is where it becomes so important that we, just like the surgical cushion in my spine, stand in the gap—aligning ourselves with the Spirit to do God-work in this world.

? I don't want Ezekiel 22:30's last statement to be about me…the
• part that says "but I found none." Will you join me and "stand in the gap," joining the Spirit, on behalf of the land?

S E N D	To.	Perry@Tyler.com
	From. . .	Mom@ABQ.com
	Subject:	Praying for Missionaries

Praying for missionaries has been my way of "standing in the gap." I am so thankful that our denomination has a prayer calendar that lists all missionaries according to their birthdays. Even those who cannot be identified because of security concerns are listed by first name or initials. For many years, as North American missionaries, our names have been on that list. Each birthday we know that thousands of people are praying specifically for us, even if they do not know us or our needs.

When you were a little boy, living with us on the Navajo reservation, you questioned why your name wasn't on the prayer calendar. You were a missionary too! Now, though your name is not individually listed, you are remembered because we pray for all chaplains each day. James wrote, "The prayer of a person living right with God is something powerful to be reckoned with" (James 5:16 TMB).

I first met them in the waiting room on the 2nd floor. They were tired from a sleepless night, but going home for some rest wasn't coming anytime soon. The accident had taken one of their children and the other had not yet regained consciousness.

She spoke first. "We've called our church and they put our daughter on the prayer-chain. My sister in Vermont called her prayer-chain and my parents said their church is praying (in California). Some friends called this morning from Michigan—they are praying." Then her husband joined the conversation, "And your brother called that prayer ministry in Florida and the one in Houston. I guess we have the whole nation praying."

The whole nation praying! What a wonderful thought. It brought them comfort and support. They knew that this crisis was not one they were enduring alone. Others were joining with them to journey through this uncertain/ unexpected/unwanted ordeal. And they weren't *just* joining them; they were remembering them before God! We have an opportunity, as God's children, to pray for others. The prayers of others can form a net that will support and hold up those in need. "Lord, listen to Your children praying."

? Who needs your prayers today? Your family? Your church? Your
• city, state and national leaders? Your friends? Someone who has abused you? Will you recommit to the important ministry of intercessory prayer?

If we were to nominate a "Now Is Fine Man of the Centuries,"
Apostle Paul would surely be declared the winner!

I think Paul could carry the title of "Or Now Is Fine Man of the Centuries,"
don't you? He definitely demonstrated his choices to obey God's "Stop!
Wait! Go!" Think about it:
  Many of his letters were written from prisons.
  He had been shipwrecked,
    Beaten, flogged and stoned,
      Misunderstood and falsely accused.
Yet over and over the concept of joy or rejoicing appears in his letters. I
believe he was saying, "Whatever your circumstances, *now is the time to…*
rejoice because you have helped others experience the joy of Christ;
  give thanks for those other believers who have blessed you;
    thank God for His indescribable gift of salvation through Christ;
      remember all that God has done for you, then
        sing praises to Him even in difficult circumstances;
          pray for those who need encouragement;
            carry all your burdens to Him, *with thanksgiving;*
              "give thanks always for everything to God the Father
              in the name of our Lord Jesus Christ."
              (Eph. 5:20 HCSB)

Remember that he was in prison, yet could write "Rejoice in the Lord
always. I will say it again: *Rejoice!*" (Phil 4:4 HCSB). That tells me that
now is the time to rejoice, not after the prison doors are opened and I am
free.

I see prisons all around me, holding captive those who did nothing to
deserve imprisonment. You know them. Prisons named:

Discouragement,
 Indecision,
  Financial burden,
   Family crisis,
    Church conflict,
     Addiction,
      Loss of or unhappiness in jobs,
       Crumbling marriages,
        Prodigal children,
         Illness.

Some of these prisons hold their captive for a few months; for some it is a life sentence without possibility of parole. Some have probably held you captive; in fact, you may still be sitting on a hard bench with the chains around your ankles.

? What prisons hold you captive? Does giving them a name help you see them from a new perspective?

? How can you glorify the Father in your circumstances?

? How can you minister to those whose prison cells are just down the hall from your own?

In all things give thanks? How about when I have something to be thankful for?
   Or Now Is Fine.
Rejoice when the diagnosis is cancer? How about when the doctor tells me I'm in remission?
   Or Now Is Fine.
Be happy while I'm suffering? You don't know how much it hurts.
   Or Now Is Fine.
Strive each day to become more like Him? But that takes so much discipline. I don't know where to begin.
   Or Now Is Fine.
Actually believing I can do *all things* through Him? Maybe someday it will happen.
   Or Now Is Fine.

Thinking only about things pure, honest, noble? Have you checked out the TV Guide lately?

Or Now Is Fine.

Placing my body, a living sacrifice, on the altar? That means dying to myself, doesn't it?

Or Now Is Fine.

Yes, accolades to Paul, the "Now Is Fine Man of the Centuries."
He was at the same time humble when thinking of himself in light of God's great love and mercy and yet confident in the power and position entrusted to him by his Master. He wholeheartedly ran the race and completed the God-given tasks he was given as best he could, through Christ's strength. He was not afraid to admit his mistakes and failures, yet he could confidently say, "Follow my example." He continually affirmed the ministries of others, always reminding them of his support with his prayers.

Will you cast your vote with mine, applying some of Paul's lessons to your own life?

- Who needs your prayers today? Write three names, then send e-mails or notes to them telling them you're praying for them. It's as simple as this: You are in my prayers.

- Will you re-adjust your thinking so that you can say in *all* things I give thanks? Make a habit of thanking God for the simplest, oft-overlooked blessings. Learn to be thankful for the chains that bind you as well as the keys that set you free.

- Each day, will you choose to look for God and how He is working in your life to create you into a person in His image? You probably won't win the "Person of the Centuries" award, but if you are able to share even one small blessing with a brother or sister along the road, I believe you will hear that awesome accolade: Well done, good and faithful servant.

Ahh, Spring Break! What pleasant memories those words hold for both me and my wife. Back in our college days, the Wayland International Choir would have Spring

Tour during this week. We would all board the bus and travel from town to town, staying in people's homes, giving concerts in churches and representing the school. It was a wonderful week. We just had to remember the "rules" for choir etiquette.

1. Dry-clean your tuxedo BEFORE and AFTER tour.
2. Eat whatever your host family serves—and like it.
3. Brush your teeth and take a shower before getting on the bus.
4. Don't do anything that reflects poorly on the school.

The list was longer…but you get the point. There was one rule, however, that we all knew, whether it was choir tour or not.

Keep your eyes on the director.

We sang some hard music. We had some difficult rhythms. We came in and cut off at different times. It would have been easy to make a mess of the music if we didn't keep our eyes on our director. Every now and then, someone would take their eyes off for a moment, and the whole choir could feel the imbalance as they held on to a note a split-second longer than the rest or didn't come in when they were supposed to. But the music was incredible when we did what we were supposed to do—keep our eyes on the director.

Sometimes life is tough. We have hard times. We feel out of rhythm with our co-workers, our friends, our families. We are finally ready to "start" and it seems everyone else is cutting off – or just the opposite. We feel out of sync and the music doesn't make sense. But, if we keep our eyes on *The Director*, He will bring amazing melodies, harmonies, blends, and precision that we can't imagine or produce on our own. Sure, there are different rules to follow for different events and times in our lives. But there is one rule that we need to hold on to…choir tour or not…

Keep your eyes on the Director!

"Let us fix our eyes on Jesus, the author and perfecter of our faith" (Heb. 12:2 NIV).

"But my eyes are fixed on You, O Sovereign LORD; in You I take refuge" (Psalm 141:8 NIV).

And suddenly, there,
   Right in the middle of the road
     Where I was traveling, it stood.
      The Mountain.
Now, what do I do?
   Strap on a backpack and climb over it?
   Be bold and assuming, and ask God to move it?
     And what if He doesn't? What then?

Turn around and go back?
Take a detour? Go around it?
Give up?
Sit down in the middle of the road
And start crying?
Because…I don't *want* this Mountain!
Thank You, Holy Father, for the Mountains in my road.
For decisions they force me to make.
For my need to depend on You as I climb up.
For my need to rejoice in You
When the Mountain is behind me.
For lessons I've learned from past Mountains,
Giving courage for ones I don't know are ahead.
Thank You, Holy Father, for the Mountains in my road.
Thank You for *this* Mountain.

Before we leave this study of Paul, let's look at him indulging in an interesting personal, and unusually intimate, conversation with the believers in Corinth. "So I wouldn't get a big head, I was given the gift of a handicap to keep me in constant touch with my limitations. Satan's angel did his best to get me down; what he in fact did was push me to my knees. No danger then of walking around high and mighty! At first I didn't think of it as a gift, and begged God to remove it. Three times I did that, *(paraphrase: Or Now Is Fine!)* and then he told me, My grace is enough; it's all you need. My strength comes into its own in your weakness. Once I heard that, I was glad to let it happen. I quit focusing on the handicap and began appreciating the gift. It was a case of Christ's strength moving in on my weakness. Now I take limitations in stride, and with good cheer, these limitations that cut me down to size—abuse, accidents, opposition, bad breaks. I just let Christ take over! And so the weaker I get, the stronger I become" (2 Cor. 12:7-10 TMB).

Whatever you wish to speculate about the handicap (or thorn, as some translations call it), the *what* is not nearly as important to me as the *why* and *how*. Paul—the man who shaped the history of Christianity in a way done by no one other than Christ Himself. Paul—the man who said, "For me to live is Christ." Paul—the premiere missionary of the Christian movement. Paul—the most prolific writer of the Bible. Was God not listening when Paul made his request? Did you ever tell your children,

"Because I said so"? Why? Because God said so. And because God had something much bigger planned for Paul.

I take heart when I think of the fact that Paul pleaded with God that the "handicap" be removed. During her 14½ year battle with cancer my mother asked, "Why, God? If I can't be healed in this life, why can't I go ahead and move into the mansion You have prepared for me?" I remember watching Jimmy's heart ache as he watched his only son fight and finally lose a 38 year "personal drug war." I hear my Uncle Oland's laugh, then recall how his addiction to alcohol literally destroyed his life and the lives of all those near to him. Just because we say "Or Now Is Fine" to God doesn't mean He is going to answer as we think or wish He would.

But I must admit I also struggle with Paul's final acceptance of the situation. As I write this I am sitting "side-saddle" at my desk. My right knee is wrapped in a brace, my leg is propped up on a footstool and my pain meds are close at hand. Bone spurs on both knees and a detached right knee cap have literally "push(ed) me to my knees." Walk around high and mighty? Ha! I can barely negotiate carefully and humbly! As a caregiver and a person who is accustomed to traveling full-speed-ahead, I am not doing well with this speed-bump. After the fall that detached the kneecap, I waited four days to learn I was scheduled for an MRI two weeks later. Then four weeks and two days after the MRI I would have an appointment with an orthopedist. *Or Now* would be a whole lot better!

Paul begged God *three times*? How about three times each day? My spiritual heart wants to agree with Paul; when I am weak, I am strong. I would like to say that I've quit focusing on the handicap and am appreciating the gift. Yes, *now* would be fine to feel that way. But reality is so constant, and pain so uncomfortable.

I emailed my miseries to a friend, and included Paul's words from these verses. She responded, "You are so amazing—finding peace and comfort in the Scriptures while in physical pain. I know it is difficult for me, yet you seem to be able to 'rise above'—what a gift and testimony you have!" Okay, God, You did it again—you pushed me down to my knees. Doesn't Linda know how weak I am? Doesn't she know that my heart is crying, "*Now,* Lord; I need some help here. I'm tired and feeling so human"? But maybe—does strength come as much in the *knowing* as in the *feeling*?

I agree more with Paul when he wrote that he had not yet attained what he could be. Lord, I want to be like You. I want to receive Your gifts—the ones I desire and the ones I would much rather forego—with grace and gratitude. I want to obey Your "Stop! Wait! Go!" directions. Help me grow to be more like You. And now would be just fine!

Our *now* and God's *now* are not in the same
time zone. Aren't you thankful He remains true to His nature,
working in His own time frame?

It doesn't take much experience of traveling through the timelines of life to realize that *our now* and *God's now* are not in the same time zone! So often we plead with God, "Now, Lord!" and He replies, "Just wait a little longer! You'll not believe the surprises I have in store for you!"

I couldn't count the number of times that I have thanked God for not being persuaded by my insistence that "*now would be just fine*," but instead remained true to Who He is, working according to His own timeframe.

Consider just a few of His promises:

"But the eyes of the Lord are on those who fear Him, on those whose hope is in His unfailing love" (Ps. 33:18 NIV).

"Those that wait upon the Lord, they shall inherit the earth" (Ps. 37:9 KJV).

"The Lord is good to those whose hope is in Him, to the one who seeks Him; it is good to wait quietly for the salvation of the Lord" (Lam. 3:25 NIV).

And of course the promise that has given hope to so many: "But they that *wait* upon the Lord shall renew their strength; they shall mount up with wings like eagles; they shall run, and not be weary, they shall walk, and not faint" (Isa. 40:31 KJV). And in his song Stuart Hamblin added, "Teach me, Lord, to wait."

Your mention of "our now" and "God's now" not being in the same time zone reminded me of a funny story that happened when we were camping last summer. Joel cracked us up! It was wonderful!

We were having so much trouble getting the camper on the ball of the hitch. This camper is always giving us trouble, even on level ground. At this campsite we were on an incline and it was just about impossible! We tried and tried, with Jordan backing up the van, then me backing up the van, then Jordan again. We were lined up right but the cap just wouldn't go all the way down on the ball. I was getting really fed-up, and grouchy, when Kelley came over (we had been trying for most of an hour) and asked, "Is there anything I can do? What do you need?" I answered, "I need a miracle," as I lowered the jack again. This time it went IMMEDIATELY onto the ball . . . smooth as silk!

We all squealed in celebration but it was Joel who was seeing it all through "heavenly" eyes. He said, "It's like all the angels were standing there, ready to run in and help, but God was saying, 'Wait for it. Wait for it.' The angels were saying, 'But he is getting so frustrated. Can't we go help him?' And God continued saying, 'Wait for it. Wait for it.' Then Momma asked what you needed and you said you needed a miracle."

"At that exact moment, God yelled, 'NOW, NOW, NOW' and the angels flew in and lowered the camper onto the van. Then God leaned back on His throne and said, 'Mission accomplished!'"

We howled with laughter. I love the way God shows Himself to children. We adults tend to miss it. But looking at your comment on timing . . . we spent all that time trying to get the hitch to work . . . asked for a miracle . . . THEN God swept in . . . so that Joel could see it from his own unique perspective!

On December 9 the doctor told me our third child would be born that evening. Call in the reinforcements (translation: mother-in-law to stay with the other two children). December 20. Cancel Christmas travel plans. December 28. Go for a "drive" on a rough jeep trail. January 1. No New Year's parties. You've heard the military statement: "Hurry up and wait"? At the time Dalton was an Army chaplain; there was no hurry up–but a lot of wait. January 3. We waited. I honestly began to wonder if I was really going to have a baby. Maybe it was a psychological pregnancy. January 5.

More waiting. Finally, on January 8, after 95 minutes of labor, Nita Lynn made her grand début at the Fort Hood hospital. *Now* had finally arrived! Bottom line, I always knew it would happen someday, though I must admit there were some moments of serious doubts!

Laura was in hard labor 43 hours. I'm sure that with each passing hour she thought Or Now Would Be *Just* Fine. Our granddaughter Alicia's water broke but she was in intense labor for almost twelve hours after. When she finally caught her breath after one especially hard contraction she reached for Jeremy's hand. "I'm sorry. I just can't do it!" she sobbed. But she did!

Even Dalton knew his drama would eventually come to an end. Surely it would. It was a cold, snowy March Saturday. A couple of shingles on the roof needed to be attached before an approaching snow storm arrived. Dalton put on the coffee, grabbed the can of tar and ladder from the garage, and headed outside. He had not been gone more than 10 minutes when the storm hit. It snowed so hard I could hardly see the car sitting in the front yard. "Boy, I'm glad he got those shingles put down before this hit." By now he would be, I was confident, safe and warm, working in the garage.

I had a cup of coffee, put on a load of laundry, turned on my stereo and sat down to write. Two cups of coffee later, with the first load of laundry in the dryer and a second load washing, I heard a constant knock-knock-knock. Maybe my washer was off balance. No; it was fine. The sound was coming from our downdraft air conditioner in the living room. Hmm, I wonder what he's doing now. I opened the back door to check on him. There, lying parallel to the house was—you guessed it—his ladder. When the storm hit, over an hour earlier, it blew the ladder down. He had banged on walls, called down drain pipes, and done anything else he thought might get my attention. There were no neighbors to help; no one was going to get out on a day like this! Jumping was not an option; the roof was much too far above the ground. Of course in New Mexico you would not expect there to be any trees nearby!

Very quickly and apologetically I stood the ladder against the wall and stepped aside, watching as my partially frozen husband slowly climbed down. Without saying a word he went into the kitchen, poured himself a still-pretty-warm cup of coffee, drank half of it and said, "From now on, when I'm out like that, you come check on me every 15 minutes."

I nodded sheepishly, trying to stifle a smile. He drank a few more sips then amended, "Make that every *ten* minutes." It was only the next day in the retelling of the story that he gradually began to grasp the humor of the situation! Even as cold (and frustrated) as he was, he did know that *eventually* someone would rescue him!

Fifteen days after the horrific January 2010 earthquake in Haiti, a sixteen year old girl was found alive. Surrounded by concrete in the bathroom of the house, she survived just over two weeks by drinking bath water. As neighbors searched through the wreckages of their homes they heard a faint cry. Rescuers were summoned; an hour later the young woman was lifted through a hole. Dehydrated, weak and barely alive, the girl managed to whisper, "Thank you."

I can almost become claustrophobic driving through a parking garage,
   Or riding through a mountain tunnel.
      Don't even think about an MRI!
I cannot begin to imagine what this young lady must have experienced
   in more than 350 hours of isolation.
     Nights that seemed as if they would never end;
       days filled with faint optimism
         that faded as the night came again,
           robbing her of any hope.
   Over and over.
     Fourteen times.
       Through aftershocks and the sounds of crumbling walls.
       "Or now" would have been more than fine –
         It would have been wonderful. But *now* did not happen.
The first few days she believed. Yes, they will find me.
   Then hope and strength both began to grow dim.
     Maybe today. Maybe tomorrow.
       But they didn't come yesterday. Why would they come today?
Now move to the world whirling around her.
   We've searched this group of houses.
     We might as well call off the search.
       No one could be alive here.
         It might be time to demolish the remaining structures.
Then, a faint cry for help.
  Now had finally come for this young Haitian woman.
     But thousands of stories did not end so well.
       Now would have been wonderful,
         but fate planned a different conclusion.

What are you experiencing today?

Are you confident that the ship really is going to reach the shore?

Even though the waiting is difficult,

The labor pains are intense,

And you think you're going to get frostbite

Can't you honestly say that sometime, some way there *will be* a conclusion?

So you aren't so sure that there is a shore out there?

The dense fog causes zero visibility.

Can you hold on just one more day?

The rescuers may be on the way.

Can you hold on even in the darkness that entombs you?

When Shadrach, Meshach and Abednego were threatened with the fiery furnace they replied,

"Our God...is able to deliver us" (Dan. 3:17-18 KJV).

"And if He doesn't?" the accusers might have asked.

"Even if He doesn't, *He is still able*" (my paraphrase).

Hang in there.

Endure the labor pains, knowing that a child *will* be born.

Zip up your coat; help *will* come sometime.

In the midst of the winter blizzard remember,

We don't say *if* spring comes; we say *when* spring comes.

"Weeping may endure for a night,

But joy *comes* in the morning" (Ps. 30:5 NKJV).

"The nights of crying your eyes out

Give way to days of laughter" (Ps. 30:5 TMB).

We were driving in late–*really* late. You have to be quiet in campgrounds when you arrive in those late night/early morning hours. With everyone asleep, both in our van (except me and my wife) and at the campground, we pulled in and set up as quickly and quietly as possible. It was rather difficult because the darkness was so thick. We couldn't see anything!

Kelley woke up first and stepped outside into the cool morning air. When she came back in she said, "You have GOT to see this." Looking out the door, I couldn't miss the sight that amazed her so. There in front of us, not more than 50 feet from our campsite, was a peaceful creek–at the base of a cliff! It was hundreds of feet high! It loomed over us, the campground, the town, the creek, and seemingly the entire world! It was beautiful. And massive! But we couldn't see it the night before. We didn't even know it was there!

We had left the Grand Canyon early the evening before. We had never been to Zion National Park. We didn't know it was quite so far–especially when you're traveling late in the day. The floor of this canyon is at the same elevation as the rim of the Grand Canyon, so when you arrive at Zion–*everything is up!*

But that's enough of the "What I did on my summer vacation" story. Here is the REAL story. God loves you. He really, really loves you. And He has promised to never leave you to face this sometimes tough world on your own. Even when you can't see Him, feel Him, sense Him. Even then, <u>especially</u> then, He is there.

In the darkest part of that night in Southern Utah we could not see anything. Sometimes our lives feel like that. We are overwhelmed. We feel lost. Our hearts ache. We can't see the cliff; we can only see the sorrow.

But when the sun comes up - - - - BAM! - - - - - WOW!!!!

That's how God is too. We can only see the darkness, the loneliness, the emptiness, the hurt, the pain, the hopelessness and the never-ending questions. "Where are you, God?!" But in His timing the sun/Son shows us a fuller picture, and we see that right there in the middle of the biggest darkness we have ever known–He is there:

Big!

Solid!

Immoveable!

Towering over all the events of our lives!

We couldn't see…but He was there all the time.

- - - - - - - - - - - - - - - - - -

A couple of nights ago two of our sons were playing a computer game; it is a program where you build your own theme park, design your own rides, decide your own admission fees, and race the "clock" to produce a successful park. They were having a blast–especially when they started building giant roller-coasters with part of the track missing, or setting the speed WAY TOO HIGH, and then testing them to watch the cars fly off the tracks and drop into the water below. The laughter was contagious. But in the middle of the laughter I started wondering–how did we ever explain life before we had theme parks?

We run around in circles like a Merry-Go-Round. We are bombarded on every side like Bumper Cars. The bottom falls out like the Parachute Drop. And then we are back to that Roller-Coaster theme every time our emotions mix and clash between the highs and lows of life.

Sometimes life can be like a 24 hour/7 day a week theme park and we can't find the exit!

But we aren't alone. It may feel lonely and overwhelming. It almost always seems as if NO ONE has ever gone through what we are experiencing. It feels like no one is there to care or hold our hand. But sit back in that Ferris Wheel seat, have another bite of cotton candy, and listen to Elijah's story.

He had major victory in his life. The prophets of Baal were defeated, the drought was over, the people even yelled out in unison, "The Lord—He is God!" Major victory. Like having your family all together and everyone's healthy. Having peace and contentment with what you're doing in life and how God is providing for your needs. Major victory.

Then his life was threatened by the Queen (she didn't appreciate his point of view). He ran and hid. Even called out to God, questioning His presence in this situation. "Hey God! Don't You see what's going on down here? Don't You even care?" Have you been there? Are you there now? You can find this story of Elijah in 1 Kings 19.

But God met him where he was, called him by name, lifted his eyes, strengthened his heart, and gave him hope. Then comes the really good part. First Kings 19:19 says, "So Elijah *went from there*..." He trusted God to be there, even when he couldn't *feel* it. And he was taken by the hand,

Led off of the Roller-Coaster,

And together - - - they found the exit.

I have today.
  It began when I woke up and got out of bed.
    It will continue in whatever direction it may go until
      It ends when I get back into bed tonight.
        I don't know what the day holds, but
I have today.
  Some things carry over from before.
    Some will continue into days ahead.
      But that is not as significant as the fact that
I have today.
  Today is a unit,
    Complete,
      Whole,
        A part of a larger unit,
          Yet complete in itself.
            Whatever else I may or may not have,

39

I have today.
　I could worry about what is ahead.
　　I could let fear of unknown stifle me.
　　　I could carry guilt,
　　　　Or frustration,
　　　　　Or regrets over what is past.
　Yesterday is gone, and I don't know
　That I will have tomorrow. But,
I have today.
　I must live it the best I can.
　　I must absorb every moment.
　　　I must find fulfillment and happiness
　　　　Wherever I can, for only for
　　　　　A few more hours do
I have today.

The singer says, "Lord help me take
　One day at a time."
Solomon said, "Do not boast about tomorrow,
　For you do not know
　　What a day may bring forth."
Jesus said, "Do not worry about tomorrow,
　For tomorrow will worry about itself.
　　Each day has enough trouble of its own."
Thank You, Holy Father, that
I have today.

Apparently Wal-Mart employees are privy to information that is not available to the general public. On a recent shopping trip we gathered our items, went to the checkout counter, and handed our money to the cashier. That's when we became aware of this imbalance of information. The cashier smiled at us, handed back some money, and said, "Here is your change."

It wasn't a matter of "when" or "where." No one questioned the "what" or "why" of it all. It was taken for granted—something that *is* going to happen. You can't run from it or ignore it. Even if you respond, "Keep it," the issue still has to be addressed– "Here is your change."

If we had been given the privilege of going through Wal-Mart orientation perhaps we wouldn't be overwhelmed by the "change" in our lives. Like the changes in the places where we work. Maybe our days wouldn't be turned upside down when a co-worker takes another position and we don't see them anymore. And the changes on the home front that follow us to work wouldn't interfere with our daily routine–things like finances (where did all these extra days come from this month?), relationships (I'm getting so much easier to live with but my spouse is becoming a grouch), children (I just enrolled them in kindergarten yesterday and today they are asking for the car keys?), and even our bodies (I'm not doing anything different but the pounds, not to mention the gray hairs, are just multiplying!).

And what's this thing with "roll-back" that they use for advertising at Wal-Mart? If that little smiley face can bump some numbers down, can it also roll-back the changes that are too high in my life?

Sometimes change is good. Sometimes change hurts so bad we can't catch our breath. It is in those times, when we have no strength and all control is lost, that we seek, with what energy we have left, to rest on something–or *Someone*.

"Jesus Christ is the same yesterday and today, <u>yes</u> and forever" (Heb. 13:8 NIV).

He **NEVER** changes.

Promises.
  A baby.
    A rosebud.
      An unwrapped package.
        An unopened door.
          A grand piano on a dark stage.
          A sealed envelope.
            A ringing phone.
Promises.
  "In my Father's house are many mansions.
    One of them is for *you!*"
  "Lo, I am with you always.
    In light and dark.
      In calm and storm."
  "I'll strengthen you, and give you power.
    For *all* power is given to Me."
  "I am able. To keep you. Till the end."
  "Be not faithless. Believe."
    "Be strong. I'll give you strength."

41

"Be calm. I'll give you peace."
  "Stand firm. I'll be your foundation."
    "Be bold. I've already won the victory!"
Promises.
  New birth.
    New chances.
      New beginnings.
        Sunrise.
          Spring.
            Today.
You make promises.
  You keep promises.
    Thank You, Lord.

The letter looked important so I decided to open it first. I plopped down in a chair in the living room to see why the State of New York had sent me this very official looking notice…only to find out that there was a warrant out for my arrest! It seems that I had failed to show up for jury duty; thus, the warrant. It was fairly easy to remedy the situation. All I had to do was mail them a copy of a utility bill showing that my residence was *indeed* in another state. No problem and no police!

This previous experience did, however, impact my response to the yellow card that came in the mail a couple of weeks ago informing me I was being summoned for jury duty in Smith County. No utility bill from Louisiana could get me off the hook this time—and I wasn't about to mess up and have another warrant issued. It just looks bad for a hospital chaplain to have such "personal" acquaintance with the law!

Everyone knows the television version of jury duty—long, difficult cases with jurors being isolated from their families and the press—but I've never met anyone who has lived that experience. All the personal stories I know are of a long, long, long day at the Court House, usually not being chosen for the jury (or perhaps just for a short case), then back on your merry way. It takes a full day but your duty is complete; you've served your time, so to speak, on the *right* side of the law.

Needless to say, that is exactly how I planned. I rearranged my schedule so that all of my Tuesday commitments were moved to Wednesday. It would make for a busy day but I would be doing my civic duty (see that pride puffing up?).

After dotting every *i* and crossing every *t*, they announced that the majority of us would be going home—our duty fulfilled. Only a few had to stay there at the Court House, except for that small group who had been chosen to take a field trip the **following morning**. This group would have to show up in a neighboring community at 10:00 a.m.

I'm sure by now you've figured out where I was appointed!

I came back to the hospital, made arrangements for coverage of my responsibilities for Wednesday morning, and moved some things to Thursday. I wasn't worried about being unable to meet those requirements for Wednesday; I was sure I'd be back in the office just like normal. After all, jury duty is always predictable…right?

"Now listen, you who say, 'Today or tomorrow we will go to this or that city, spend a year there, carry on business and make money.' <u>Why, you do not even know what will happen tomorrow</u>" (James 4:13-14 NIV).

Our calling is not to "plan" tomorrow, but to be obedient and faithful today.

═ ═ ═ ═ ═ ═ ═ ═ ═ ═ ═ ═ ═ ═

Hey, Noah, when is the right time to start building an ark?
   When you see the lightning? Hear the thunder?
      What you feel the first drops of rain?
         How about when God first says, "Do it!"?
Hey, Abraham, when is the right time to begin your journey?
   When God outfits your camels with On Star?
      Or sends you a Tom Tom?
         After Sarah has given birth to Isaac?
         How about when God says,
           "Go to a land that I will show you!"?
Hey, Jonah, when is the right time to preach to Nineveh?
   After you've been thrown overboard?
      After an Encounter of the Worst Kind with a fish?
         How about when God says, "Arise! Go to Nineveh!"?
Hey, Sarah, when is the right time to start knitting baby blankets?
   When you are having morning sickness?
      After you feel the first contractions of labor?
         How about as soon as the angel announces,
           "Yeah, Girl! It's a *boy!*"?
Hey, Mary, when do you become the mother of God's Son?
   When you place His tiny body in the manger?
      When you see His bloody, bruised body hanging on the cross?
         How about the moment you say,

"Your handmaiden is willing"?
Hey, Peter, when is it the right time to step out of the boat
    And onto the water?
        After the waves have died down and you can see a rock?!
            When you have one hand on the boat rail and the other in His?
                How about when you ask "Lord, is that really *You*?"
                    And He answers, "Come!"?
Hey, Young Woman, when is the right time to follow God's plan for
your life?
    After you complete your education and begin a career?
        After you follow your heart's dream?
            How about when God says, "This is the path I have chosen for
you!"?
 Hey, Handsome Couple, when is the right time to serve Christ in another country?
    After your children are in college and your retirement is secure?
        After you are proficient in three languages?
    How about when God says,
        "Now! Here's where I want *you* to serve *Me!*"?

Faith without doubting.
    Obedience without hesitating.
        Trust without faltering.
            Action without questioning.

But what if Noah had feared the laughter of his neighbors?
    What if Abraham had never taken that first step away from home?
        What if Jonah had never gotten on that boat in the first place?
            What if Sarah had feared that the pain was too great?
                What if Mary had said, "No way!"
                    And Peter had feared the rough, deep water?
                        What if Lottie Moon had said, "I can't go to China!" and
                            No young couples obeyed God's call
                                to leave their homelands with the Gospel?
But Noah *did* build, Abraham *did* move,
    And Jonah did finally obey God's voice.
        Sarah and Mary both had the bouncing baby boys,
            And Peter walked on water–well, almost!
                And thousands of missionaries have taken God's love

44

"to the ends of the earth."
When God says "build," now is fine.
   When He says "Go" and when He says "Come," now is fine.
      When He says "Bear the pain,"
         "Speak the Word," "Share My love,"
            Now is the time to obey.
"I know what I'm doing. I have it all planned out—plans to take care of you, not abandon you, plans to give you the future you hope for. When you call on me, when you come and pray to me, I'll listen. When you come looking for me, you'll find me. Yes, when you get serious about finding me and want it more than anything else, I'll make sure you won't be disappointed" (Jer. 29:11-14 TMB).

We must have listened to the song on that cassette a thousand times. The tempo was upbeat, the tune was catchy, the words were powerful–and memorable.

Never-the-less–I do confess You are the Light of my way
Never-the-less, whatever the test, I'm gonna trust, Trust and Obey.

He was a celebrated war hero, but he was covered with leprosy. She was a slave, but she talked of a prophet. He didn't like the task he was given, but Naaman dipped in the muddy Jordan River and came out clean. Cured. Healed. Humbled. He obeyed... *never-the-less.*

Abraham was given the son of God's promise and now he didn't understand this command to sacrifice him. He didn't know he would receive him back, but he obeyed...*never-the-less.*

Moses ran away, chased sheep through the wilderness, and spoke with a stutter, but marched back with God's message for Pharaoh to let the Israelites go. He didn't want to go back to Egypt, but he obeyed...*never-the-less.*

The song we liked so much ended with the words to a hymn that you may know:

Trust and Obey, For there's no other way,
To be happy in Jesus, but to Trust and Obey.

"Trust and Obey" looked great for Naaman, Abraham, and Moses. Big success followed their obedience. But it isn't always easy and it doesn't always turn out the way we might want it.

Daniel put T&O into practice and ended up in a lion's den.

Elijah put T&O into practice and was chased out of town by a wicked queen.

Jesus put T&O into practice and was nailed to a cross.

God never promised life would look like we want it to look. He never promised that there would only be major successes. He didn't promise we would always be happy.

He promised to always be with us. To fill us with unspeakable joy because we know Who holds the outcome. He promised to be faithful. Our task...to *trust and obey!* Period.

You may be looking around at the broken things in your world right now, but will you join me in believing and putting our trust in the impossible? Will you join me by following His voice even if it doesn't make sense? Remember—Daniel wasn't lion chow, Elijah heard the still, small voice of God, and Jesus beat the tar out of death.

Will you trust and obey - - - *never-the-less?*

SEND	To.	Perry@Tyler.com
	From. . .	Mom@ABQ.com
	Subject:	Trust and Obey

Thanks for reminding me of this special song. I had felt as a young child that God was calling me to serve Him as a missionary. I became church pianist my second year of high school. One evening as we sang "Trust and Obey" I knew that I must acknowledge His call publicly. I played as the congregation sang the first verse, then as the second verse began I left the piano and went to Bro. Rich, sharing my commitment with him. There was no doubt to everyone there that night what was happening!

Remember the old Burger King jingle? The commercial showed smiling BK employees happily making burgers while they sang,

"Hold the pickles, hold the lettuce; special orders don't upset us. All we ask is that you let us serve it YOUR way. Have it your way, at Burger King. Have it your way."

Our order looks like this:

"I'd like the 8 piece chicken tenders, no sauce."

"I'd like a Whopper with cheese, no pickles or onions."

"Make mine a combo meal with French fries."

"Me too—but with onion rings."

46

"And a Diet Coke."

"I guess I'll have the same, a Diet Coke, since my doctor told me I can't have REAL Coke anymore."

What about your order? Did you take the hamburger right off the menu—no changes, no substitutions? And now...did you feel justified making those changes—with no guilt at all—because that is what Burger King stands for and those are our rights as American citizens?

What else can you think of where you deserve to "have it your way"?

Your car?

Your yard?

Your hair style?

Your _Bible_?

Yep, that's where we can come pretty close to messing up the whole burger! We feel so justified (and we are so used to it) that we believe we have the right to pick and choose what fits us best.

"God is Love – so everyone goes to heaven, right?"

"I like the 'Mother Hen' reference—so why do we stick with this old-fashioned, gender reference of 'Father'?"

"I don't think this (particular action) is so wrong. I mean, come on, God MADE me this way."

Second Timothy 3:16 says, "All Scripture is God-breathed..."

All. Not some. I can't take Matthew and Romans but leave off Proverbs and Acts. All. The full thing. Lettuce, tomatoes, pickles, mustard, mayonnaise, cheese, sesame seed bun, flame-broiled patty, and even onions. All.

There may be parts I don't understand. There may be parts I wish weren't there because they convict me about my own actions. There may be parts that I just overlook because they seem bland. But I am not given the option to "have it your way" and take something out. I didn't write the book or speak the words.

"All Scripture is God-breathed and is useful for teaching, rebuking, correcting and training in righteousness, so that the man of God may be thoroughly equipped for every good work" (2 Tim. 3:16 NIV).

He has a purpose, and it's not all about me having MY way—no matter how many options there are on the Burger King menu—or I may hope to find in my Burger King Bible.

"It has occurred to me that many, many wonderful things
    Have happened in my life
        For which I was so completely unprepared.
            Too insensitive,
                Too ignorant,
                    Too frivolous,
    That their full significance never struck me
        Until years later, or perhaps never.
    Possibly this has happened to you, too.
        If so, then this Christmas season is for us:
            For you and me."

Several years ago I received a Christmas letter with those words, which
prompted me to write the following:
I realize that as I walk through life
    I come upon so many truly great events purely by accident.
We plan for weddings,
    For the birth of children,
        For moves and career changes.
But we chance to meet a person
    And our lives are changed forever.
We chose to take a side trail
    And our lives are never again the same.
We fall, and receive a wound
    That takes a lifetime to heal.
We say "yes" to a new challenge
    And a world of opportunities is ours.
We see a flower, stop to smell it,
    And discover it is one of the rarest flowers in the world.
We say, "I'll see you tomorrow."
    And we never see that friend again.
People went to a ball game in San Francisco
    And experienced an earthquake.
A parade. Smiles. Waves. A shot.
    The President was dead.
A theater audience was annoyed when the movie they went to see
    Was cancelled so they could preview a new movie:
        "Gone with the Wind."
Shepherds watched their sheep as they had done for centuries.

48

And they heard the Angels sing!
Glory to God in the Highest! And on earth – peace.
Lord, help me keep my eyes open so I will
Recognize these moments when they come.
Help me keep a feeling of excitement and
Anticipation so that every day,
Every moment
May be one of the best, the greatest,
That I have yet lived.

It was the first time I can remember having Tater Tots. I didn't really like them, but they were so different…and that matters when you're a kid.

We were at the home of some family friends. The kind of "family friends" where you can't remember a time when they were NOT a part of your life. Apart from the whole tater-tot-experience, most of my memories of Bob are of him sitting in our living room, talking with my parents until late into the night, his distinct voice occasionally waking me up from sleep. Could it really be 2:00 a.m. and they are still up? I thought my parents were too old to be able to do that!!!

And yet yesterday his wife, Karen, wrote to my parents and told them that Bob has multiple myeloma. Now I'm thinking that he, my parents, and anyone else with the "c" word, are way too YOUNG to be carrying such a load (whatever their age may be). Why do people have to have such deep heartache? Why do folks have to deal with life-threatening illness, constant visits to the doctor, learning a new clinical language that was so foreign just weeks ago? Why do Tater Tots suddenly sound like such a wonderful memory that I can literally smell them cooking in the kitchen?

Please take a moment and read some words I pulled out of Karen's e-mail message:

"We are blessed greatly with our doctors. The radiologist still holds his MD Anderson affiliation and was a teacher of radiology there before he came here to head our new radiology cancer center. Our hematologist is new here and is a very published cancer researcher, our ENT is also incredible. All three have seen the nasal presentation before, which is extremely rare, about 10 cases a year in the US. So we are in their capable hands, but the hands that count the most are His hands.

"Anyway, it is very bad and I am not hopeful unless the Lord chooses to do a miracle. I think that is not going to happen as he gave me a Scripture repeatedly for almost 6 months before we found out about this so I knew something was

going to happen. He has lovingly prepared me with His word and I am trying to rest in Him and know the future is secure in His loving hands."

Why do we have such heartache? Perhaps part of the reason is so that we won't allow the "c" word...cancer...to overshadow another "C" word–the Christ who comforts/strengthens/challenges us with memories of His presence in our lives. So that we can say, with feeble voice and tear-stained cheeks, we are "lovingly prepared" and we are "in capable hands, but the hands that count the most are His hands."

"See, I (God speaking) have engraved you on the palms of My hands" (Isa. 49:16a NIV).

Memories are precious and are to be cherished. There are so many things we need to remember, and *now is the time* to remember, while we can.

My daughter Rhonda and I were discussing a movie we both enjoy. She said, "I have seen it at least a dozen times, but it's like meeting an old friend! It's just good to remember!" Memories are precious and are to be cherished. Often it is only in the remembering that we see how God was plotting and directing our journey. My dear friend Ed cannot remember his home address or phone number, who is standing beside him in the picture or his daughter's name. There are so many things we need to remember, and *now is the time* to remember, while we can.

Over and over in the Old Testament God commanded His children to "Stop! Remember!" Then when He gave the call to move forward, they could do so confidently, recalling His provisions and guidance in the past. The very same principles and promises holds true for us.

Scrapbooking is the craft of the day. Why? To preserve those precious memories. Remembering helps us:
Know that when things seem the darkest, the light will eventually shine through.

Believe that joy *will* come in the morning; it always has before.

Walk through the deep valleys of life,
Knowing we will eventually rest beside still waters.
Find strength to go on
When we are sure we have taken our last step.
Understand who we are, Whose we are,
Where we came from,
And the difference it all has made in our lives.

As they sat around the table talking and laughing about the events of the day, He leaned over, grabbed some of the bread, raised it up, and broke it. This wasn't so unusual–He always took the bread first and asked God's blessing on it. But this time, when He broke the bread, He said, "Remember Me." What did it mean? What was He saying?

The disciples did not understand all that Jesus was saying that night. But later, after they saw Him alive again, His message began to make sense. Things that He had taught them came to mind with clarity. Some of those things had been confusing, even hard to swallow. But now they understood. Now they remembered. And the memories gave them comfort and strength. The memories brought them together as a group. And they are just as powerful today as then…"remember Me."

Some memories can bring pain. Peter's memory of denying Christ, the beatings that tore into Jesus' flesh, the horrible death on a cross would all be unpleasant. But others would be wonderful! Like the feeding of such a huge crowd with only 5 loaves of bread and 2 fish, walking on water, and just enjoying the company of someone they all loved so deeply.

Memories are the same for us. Some are painful and others very pleasant. All are needed. Memories allow us to cry, laugh, grow and heal. Without them, we would lose the strength we have gained from past experiences. We would miss out on the laughs that come from the silliness of life. We would have a much more lonely existence.

Remembering is a good idea. It may bring tears. In fact, if the memory is painful, it probably will. Or, folks may look at you and wonder why there is that goofy smile on your face. Just count it as another opportunity to celebrate a remarkable gift…the gift of remembering…and share the story with someone–if you're able.

Christ broke bread and said "remember." Let's "feast" on the blessings gained from our memories and praise the One who called us to hold those memories near.

What does the "Lord's Supper" or communion if you prefer, mean to you personally? Jesus said, "When you do this, remember Me." I remember the awe I felt when, after my baptism just before my ninth birthday, I had the privilege of being a part of this special time as I sat between Mama and Daddy. I recall the time when, as church pianist, I was playing a worshipful meditation as the elements were being passed. My daddy, who always wore cowboy boots, stepped up onto the platform right beside me…but his foot was not completely on the platform and it slipped back to the floor with a "thud." Startled, I am afraid my music only added to the excitement of watching those cups of grape juice dance gleefully in the air!

While Dalton was an army chaplain we worshiped with believers from a variety of backgrounds and faiths. During his one-year tour of duty in Vietnam he offered the Lord's Supper to military personnel at their home base as well as at many field locations, landing zones and Green Beret camps. As missionaries on the Navajo reservation, we frequently observed communion with fellow believers there. I have "remembered Him" with believers in Zimbabwe, Thailand and Brazil. Groups of worshipers have numbered from hundreds to handfuls. Occasions have been worship services, those on special occasions such as Christmas and New Year's Eve, and once at a funeral. One of our pastors asked new believers to be seated on the front row during their first experience of taking the Lord's Supper and he personally served them.

Several years ago our pastor made a trip to the Holy Land and brought back olive wood communion cups for all his church family. The following Sunday morning he announced that during the evening service we would be observing the Lord's Supper then we could each take our cup home as a souvenir. With anticipation we received our juice-filled cups as they were handed to us. Following the pastor's instruction to drink from the cup, all those in the congregation almost caught their breath as they tasted the bitter juice. The next Sunday morning our pastor offered his apologies! The deacons prepared the cups immediately after the morning service, completely unaware that the juice would absorb the bitter taste from the olive wood!

More recently two of our church staff members came to our home on a Monday afternoon. Because of Dalton's poor health he had been unable to attend church for several months. At one o'clock W. A. and Ted came to our home, carrying several communion cups, pieces of bread, and a 48 ounce bottle of grape juice! As the four of us sat around our dining room table, once again "doing this in remembrance of Him," we shared a very special time of fellowship.

Remembering Him, what He has done in our lives, the ways He has led us—makes all the difference. It is good, not only to reflect on what He did for us in His death, but also the bond of fellowship this act created for us as His disciples. Whether with a body of fellow believers or alone with your Master, do this in remembrance of Him.

I was listening to the radio on my way to the hospital. They were putting callers on the air, allowing them to tell stories of the military folks they wanted to honor on that day–Veterans Day. There were wonderful, tear-jerking stories, interwoven with patriotic songs, which were shared as reminders of standing up for beliefs, strength, unselfish giving, honor, and courage. And I began remembering.

I am not in any way trying to minimize the importance of Veterans Day and those who have served in our country's military, but my mind went to some "Veterans" of another battle–a spiritual battle.

I thought about Mr. Armstrong, who was older than Noah when I first met him, and the faithfulness he showed by his involvement and attendance in the church of my childhood. Whenever we would have those "congregation choice" hymns, he would choose the same one: "Are Ye Able." And I can still hear his voice singing (he stood right behind us!), "Lord, we are able. Our spirits are Thine. Remold us, make us, like Thee divine." And I remember the actions I saw in this man who stood up for his beliefs!"

I thought about Thomas Griffith, who was a GIANT of a man (the tallest man I'd ever seen) and his faithfulness in teaching a bunch of rowdy boys in Sunday school. This man who was big in stature showed us the shortest verse in the Bible–"Jesus wept" (John 11:35 NIV), and I saw his heart flow with compassion over the brokenness of others when they were hurting. And I remember the picture of true strength–not his own but the Christ who lived in him!

I thought about Verne Campbell, who was willing to put action to his faith and words, and take on the responsibility of raising my sisters and myself IF anything had ever happened to my parents while we were growing up. We always knew this was a "second father," willing to play the role because he followed the voice of his Heavenly Father. And I remember that unselfish giving builds great relationships!

I thought about Bro. Long, our pastor, who stood faithfully on God's Word, holding it in such high esteem. He constantly reminded us to do the same–cherish the Word of God in print and in Person. And I remember that he lived his life as an example of commitment and honor to Christ in front of us as a group of distracted high-schoolers!

And I thought about Dalton Edwards, my dad, who has faithfully served, followed, honored, and loved the God he knew as a Father. (You see, he lost his own dad when he was still young.) He continued following when God moved him to the lonely remote back corners of the Navajo Reservation to remind those shepherds of the Great Shepherd. He continued serving when ethnic pastors needed someone who also understood their culture to help train them in Scripture. He continued supporting when ministry-focus moved from his shoulders to the shoulders of my mother as she stepped into a missions training role. And he continues faithfully acknowledging the Great Physician as he lives with a life-threatening disease. And I remember his courage to walk in the steps of The Master, even when he didn't know where they would lead.

Praise God for those who have served in the military and for a special day to honor them. But also take the opportunity to praise God for the "veterans" of the faith, those who have gone before us to show us the path of following God—reminders of standing for their beliefs, strength, unselfish giving, honor, and courage.

We are truly surrounded and blessed by a "great cloud of witnesses" (Heb. 12:1 NIV).

You know those V-8 commercials where someone gets bonked on the forehead because they just don't "get it"? I've had God do that to me a few times—a couple of them recently. You see, I'm a visual learner. What that means is that I have to "see" it to really be able to comprehend it.

So I think it is very, very cool that God makes allowances for those of us that He created this way, as we see in Ephesians 2:7,

"...in order that...He (God) might SHOW the incomparable riches of His grace."

In 1990 we were blessed with the birth of a little boy—in order that God might show the incomparable riches of His grace! He was so small, so helpless, so precious, so wonderful. And I knew that I would NEVER let anyone or anything ever hurt him. I would protect him with every ounce of strength I had. I would die for him—but would absolutely NEVER give him to die for someone else. And in that priceless little person I saw the depth of God's love—that He would send His son to take on human flesh, to leave eternity to deal with the limitations of time, to move from Creator to created, so that we would have a Savior/Redeemer who knew what it was like to live with the temptations and struggles of this world—so that we would have a High Priest who could identify with our suffering—so that we, by placing our trust in Him, could become children of God.

Eighteen years later, that same little boy graduated from High School—in order that God might show the incomparable riches of His grace! He wore a graduation cap with a bright tassel, not a crown of thorns. He had colorful cords draped around his shoulders to show his high academic achievements, not cords lashed across his flesh, ripping through skin and muscle leaving him unrecognizable. He gave a speech, with joy in his voice, about the blessings and honor that God had bestowed—not crying out, with pain and loneliness in his voice, wondering why God had forsaken him. He cheered with his classmates when his teachers and school administrators said, "It is finished." And in that grown-up boy I saw the depth of God's love—that His Son completed the work of the cross, crying out, "It is finished," receiving death instead of a diploma—giving us an incredible gift while we were at our very worst. "But God demonstrates His own love for us in this: While we were still sinners Christ died for us" (Romans 5:8 NIV).

As I write these words, this same son is actively involved in his college experience—in order that God might show the incomparable riches of His grace! It was not "finished" with the completion of high school. It was not "finished" when Jordan turned 18. It was not "finished" when he moved out of the house and enrolled in college two states away. In fact, it looks like it is just starting! And in this young man I see the depth of God's love that He didn't "finish" at the cross—He "started" by coming out of the tomb! He defeated death, He conquered sin, He is seated at God's right hand, and is preparing a home for all His followers where we will be with Him for eternity. Life has been given freely and fully!

Over the years it has taken a little baby wrapped in a blue blanket to remind me that another little baby, placed in a manger, was indeed the Messiah—in order to show the incomparable riches of His grace!

Why celebrate **special occasions** just at the "proper" time, when they can be a blessing to us throughout the year? Now Is Fine!

S E N D	To.	Perry@Tyler.com
	From. . .	Mom@ABQ.com
	Subject:	Special Occasions

Recently, on a warm summer morning, Cheryl began playing the prelude to the next hymn. Did I hear correctly? Were we really going to sing "Joy to the World"? In the *summer?* Well, why not? Why should we limit our memories and celebration of special occasions just to those times when they can be a blessing to us throughout the year? We could wait till the "proper" time to celebrate, but hey, Or Now Is Fine! Also, remembering special days and seasons can be springboards for giving us insights and ideas throughout the year.

Several of your Faith Boosts were written on a variety of these occasions. I think "Now Is Fine" ☺ for including some of them, okay? And what better place to begin than with a New Year!

The start of a new year—for some, there is excitement over the "newness" of life and the opportunity for changes or growth. For others, it is just another day—December 31 and January 1 look a lot alike with the same old stuff hanging around to be dealt with each day.

In the 21st chapter of the Gospel of John, we read these words: Simon Peter, Thomas, Nathanael from Cana in Galilee, the sons of Zebedee, and two other disciples were together. "I'm going out to fish," Simon Peter told them, and they said, "We'll go with you."

See, Simon Peter was a fisherman by trade. That's what he was doing when Jesus called him. It's what he knows. It's what he can fall back on when everything falls apart—when he doesn't know what to do next—when he's scared about stepping forward—or when he doesn't know HOW to step forward. Jesus had been crucified. There was this big stir on the third day and some women said the guys ought to check it out. Peter raced to the tomb, found it empty (like his heart), but didn't understand. So here we have Peter going back to what he knows, and taking others with him. Pull out your Bible and finish reading those verses in John 21. Jesus shows up and sets everything on course. Wow! What it must have been like to be in Peter's shoes that day!

Now turn the page in your Bible and begin the first chapter of Acts. Jesus has been with the disciples for 40 days after the Resurrection. He gives some final instructions and then, as verse 9 tells us, He was taken up before their very eyes, and a cloud hid Him from their sight. That's cool! But what follows is even more cool (for us today)! "They were looking intently up into the sky as He was going, when suddenly two men dressed in white stood beside them. 'Men of Galilee,' they said, 'why do you stand here looking into the sky? This same Jesus, who has been taken from you into heaven, will come back in the same way you have seen Him go into heaven'" (Acts 1:10-11 NIV).

Catch the first part— "why are you just standing here wasting time, hands in your pockets, sky-gazing?" Ok, maybe it wasn't worded exactly like that, but you get the message. Jesus told them He is returning, the angels reminded them He is returning, and we have the promise today…He is returning! We don't need to train our focus on the past (going back to fishing, whatever "fishing" may be for you) —we need to be looking forward! We have a Jerusalem, all Judea and Samaria, and to the ends of the earth (v. 8) to be thinking about.

It is important—powerfully important—to remember what God has done for us. But I don't think we should wallow, dwell, camp out, build a cabin, put down roots, and plan on digging in to STAY in the past. It didn't work for Peter and the other disciples and it doesn't work well for us. Let's join the apostle Paul and "forgetting what is behind and straining (pressing on) toward what is ahead." Let's not be caught just standing around sky-gazing in the New Year.

Did you set any New Year's resolutions for yourself this year? How are they going so far? Since it is so common for us, in our culture, not to maintain consistency with our resolutions, I have decided I am making some this year that I am pretty sure I can keep. Here is my list:

Gain more unwanted weight.

Eat too much sugar and saturated fats.

Think about beginning an exercise routine.

Be more consistent in maintaining my resolutions.

Celebrating a new beginning usually fills us with big dreams and plans. I don't think there is anything wrong with us approaching something new that way. Otherwise, we would be bored and depressed. Think about the excitement of a new job, a new child joining the family, a new project around the house that you have been looking forward to for years and the time is finally here to complete it. The list goes on and on.

Where we tend to struggle is when we don't fulfill our dreams and plans. If things don't turn out the way we hope for, we feel like failures. The problem with this type of thinking is that it is filled with too much "me."

I can't make this a perfect year. I can't make the sun rise or the wind blow. I can't slow the years down or even add one day to my life. I can *think* about new beginnings but I can't *make* new beginnings, not the really important things. But there is hope—because I know the One Who can.

"In the beginning was the Word, and the Word was with God, and the Word was God. He was with God in the beginning. Through Him all things were made; without Him nothing was made that has been made. In Him was life, and that life was the light of men" (John 1:1-4 NIV).

LIFE…now *that* is a beginning to celebrate!

****The following messages are extremely private and must only be read by those for whom they are addressed. Do NOT attempt to decipher the specially coded message intended for the opposite gender, as pain and confusion may result.****

FOR MEN ONLY: Girl Holiday coming up! Begin planning immediately! Must include red hearts, corny lines from chick flicks, and food (in most cases—**NOT** chips from the bag!).

FOR WOMEN ONLY: After months and months of preparation, that special man in your life is going to honor you on Valentine's Day as only he can—so be forgiving and patient!

Ahhh, Valentine's Day. Celebrated pretty much the same around the nation: a card, a special dinner, some chocolate, and a gift showing our affection.

In New York City—handmade original card by a calligrapher in Greenwich Village, dinner at Tavern On The Green, a heart-shaped box of Godiva chocolates with the center piece of candy replaced by diamond jewelry.

In Hollywood–a Microsoft e-card delivered to your door by Bill Gates, a private jet to New England for Maine Lobster, then Switzerland for artisan designed chocolates, with a stop in NYC for a trinket from Tiffany's.

In Texas– "I Love You" written across the sky from horizon to horizon by a small airplane, a horseback ride to your favorite Tex-Mex restaurant for Fajitas, a chocolate milkshake or dipped cone at Diary Queen, and new boots…red leather.

And the next morning only two things remain–the smell of onions on your clothes from that steaming skillet of fajitas, and a pair of red boots that will go in the back of the closet until next Valentine's Day, along with the red cowboy hat you received the year before. The thought was nice; it was a fun evening, but it's gone too soon.

The Samaritan woman liked those nights. They made her feel special. She loved the attention, the gifts, the fancy dinners. But her everyday life was empty, so she bounced from man to man–marrying and leaving five of them before settling on her present boyfriend. Until the day she went to the well for some water and met Jesus, and He offered something deeper; something she was really looking for in the middle of the trinkets and chocolate. He offered her "Living Water" –forgiveness, acceptance, unconditional love–the promise that she would "thirst no more" (see John 4).

Valentine's Day is wonderful and fun. I am thankful for all the years I've had to celebrate with my special Valentine and I hope I am able to celebrate many more years with her. But I'm even more thankful that God loves me (and my Valentine) with a love that is beyond understanding and lasts much longer than the smell of grilled onions and leather boots!

In a popular reality television show contestants sing each week, competing in front of a panel of judges. Viewers called in their vote for their favorite. One of the consistent pieces of advice that is given is over the song choice. The judges may like the voice, the band, the clothing, the hair. They may like the singer as a personal favorite, but they may not agree that the contestant's choice of song "fit" them for their style and ability.

Let's take a look at the song choice of three men. You might remember the song sung and written by Dallas Holm, "Rise Again." King David wrote/sang Psalm 22. Jesus was the Inspiration for both!

Go ahead, drive the nails in my hands
    ("they have pierced my hands and my feet"—v. 16 NIV)
Laugh at me where you stand
    ("all who see me mock me; they hurl insults"—v. 7 NIV)

Go ahead and say it isn't me
("scorned by men and despised by the people"—v. 6 NIV)
The day will come when you will see
("all the ends of the earth will remember and turn to the LORD, and all the families of the nations will bow down before Him"—v. 27 NIV)
Cause I'll Rise Again
("for **He has done it!**"—v. 31 NIV)

Incredible song choice, wouldn't you say? "Speak to one another with psalms, hymns and spiritual songs. Sing and make music in your heart to the Lord" (Eph. 5:19 NIV). Keep singing!

Our family had to make some changes the first year we lived in Texas. **Major** changes!! Mother's Day came too late! It totally threw off everything that the kids and I know about celebrating this special day. That is, of course, with the consideration that we are a house full of boys, with the exception of the youngest, and we guys don't make changes easily.

Here is the reason for the changes. We moved to Texas from Nebraska and everyone knows that you can't plant before May 15th. Well, you CAN plant–but it will freeze. So we wait until after the 15th and then folks start adding beautiful flowers to their yards and the farmers get out in the fields. Here was the problem. For many years I took the kids to pick out the flowers that they want to give Mom for planting in the yard. We didn't know all of the names of the flowers–we just picked the style and colors that we knew Mom liked. Then, on Mother's Day, we would bring all our flowers in and cover the table with them, waiting for Mom to walk into the kitchen to see her "surprise." You see–she loves to plant flowers!

But not this year. Oh no! THIS year the flowers were in the ground nearly TWO MONTHS before Mother's Day came around. How can you pick out flowers when the garden is already full? And we certainly couldn't ask Mom to wait on putting in her garden. (Did I already mention–she loves to plant flowers?!) So we had to make changes. Major changes. And they come slowly to us men.

It reminded me of another argument over a "day" on the calendar. The Pharisees were upset that Jesus' disciples were plucking heads of grain on the Sabbath and eating them. They fussed at Jesus, looking for a reason to discredit Him, and His response was, "The Sabbath was made for man, not man for the Sabbath. So the Son of Man is Lord even of the Sabbath." (You can find the story in Mark 2:23-28.)

The Pharisees needed to see that the Sabbath was given TO men for their time of worship and rest. The day is a gift–not a burden with all its laws and rules to trip us up and make us feel worthless before God. He wants to be our Lord, to celebrate time and relationship with each other, not to have us bound up in ritual to a day—which makes the <u>day</u> more important than the <u>Lord of the day</u>.

So, as I said, we had to make major changes our first Mother's Day in Texas. We had to see Mom as more important than the "day" and change our pattern of gift-giving. (Which, of course, was not difficult to do—she is pretty special!) We also had to accept that the flowers were in the ground when we were used to frost.

And we were reminded that the "days" are a gift from God, given that we might be in relationship with Him on each and every one of them—not binding us up and sticking us in a box to waste away while we make them fit OUR schedule.

Today (yes, THIS day) celebrate the Lord of the Sabbath!

For our gang, in some ways it was a typical July 4th celebration: family, homemade ice cream, a community fireworks display. In other ways it was unusual: brisket instead of hot dogs and hamburgers, fines for shooting off personal fireworks, and shorter, quick-burning sparklers.

But some things remain true year after year: remembering freedom; remembering the price paid to get us to where we are today; remembering sacrifice.

In some ways it was a typical Independence Day: loved ones sitting around the table, the traditional meal being served, anticipation of the upcoming celebration.

In other ways it was unusual: broken bread called His body, a shared cup called His blood. And then He spoke: "Remember!"

Every time you eat this bread remember the battle. Remember the war that took place with heaven's throne as the prize. Remember the sacrifice.

Every time you drink this cup remember the price paid. Remember the Declaration of Independence: "It is finished!" (Death is defeated and has no more hold on us.) Remember freedom.

It was unusual that God would take our place and accept such tremendous torture on our behalf.

It should be typical that we remember a gift of freedom that we cannot provide for ourselves.

Independence Day. HE IS RISEN!! Remember.

"Give thanks in all circumstances for this is God's will for you in Christ Jesus" (1 Thess. 5:18 NIV).

We have a tradition in our family. It isn't original or unique in any way. There are many families who share this tradition. When we sit down to eat our Thanksgiving Dinner we go around the table and each person, regardless of age, shares the things for which they are thankful.

Some things are what you would expect during this time of reflection.
  "I'm thankful for my family."
    "I'm thankful for health."
      "I'm thankful for this special day and for all of us being together."
        "I'm thankful for Jesus."
Others are more concrete.
  "I'm thankful for my teddy bear."
    "I'm thankful for my bike."
      "I'm thankful for pumpkin pie with _lots_ of whipped topping."
Still others have hidden messages.
  "I'm thankful not all of the pies were burned."
    "I'm thankful for the help I'll have washing the dishes."

What a gift it is to have a specific day set aside for us to give thanks. The day reminds us to celebrate the events/ordeals where God has placed us and the many lives that have touched us (and that we have touched) over the year. But we often lose sight of it in our daily living because some things don't automatically bring forth "Thanksgiving".

However, the above scripture doesn't say we have to _be_ thankful FOR the circumstances…those things that really rub us the wrong way!

It says _give_ thanks IN all circumstances. Not "thanks" that He gives us events that only bring good and not sorrow. Instead, "thanks" that He gives us Himself.

And that develops an attitude, and expression, of thanks that admits things may be hard, but God is good!

"Know that the Lord is God.
  It is He who made us, and we are His;
    We are His people, the sheep of His pasture.
Enter His gates with thanksgiving and His courts with praise;
  Give thanks to Him and praise His name.
    For the Lord is good and His love endures forever;
      His faithfulness continues through all generations"
        (Psalm 100:3-5 NIV).

There were so many unusual things surrounding this "holiday" birth:
An unmarried couple.

Giving birth in a community that was not their hometown.

A rushed flight in the middle of the night to save the baby's life.

The visit from a messenger dressed in a white robe.

The messenger spoke to the father. It felt like a dream, but he knew it was real. The words were simple. "We did everything we could, but your daughter died."

It was not the joyful celebration that they were expecting, that they wanted, that they had dreamed about and planned for all these months. The room was ready and waiting. Why this? Why now? Why their baby? Why them?

During this time of the year when we focus on another holiday birth, Jesus the Messiah coming as a baby who was laid in a manger, we almost feel entitled to happiness. We think there shouldn't be pain, sadness, misery, tears, loss of hope, or death. Especially for babies.

But the world doesn't deal in "fair." Justice is still tainted. Hope is crushed more often than not. Pain comes daily and tears are much more common than we prefer. We don't have all the answers and we wish we never had to ask some of the questions that burst from our hearts and souls. Deep questions. "Why" questions.

And THAT is why we celebrate birth during this time of year. THAT is why we read of angel announcements when the white robe we see is on a doctor. THAT is why we sing of silent nights when our nights are filled with soul-screams and sobs. THAT is why we celebrate, not with false expectations, but with real hope. Because a "holiday baby" was born to save us from sin, to give us a future that is glorious, to heal brokenness that we can't fix, to give us hope…when there seems to be none.

He came into our very real, broken, dirty world, with all its hurts and pains, to carry pain with and for us. He came, Immanuel, so we would know God is with us. He came to carry "holiday" birth dreams that are crushed so we could know that there is more to life.

"For unto us a child is born, unto us a son is given"

(Isaiah 9:6 KJV).

He came.

Grief is difficult during the holidays. It is also much more common than we may want to admit. You don't have to hang around any public place for very long before you hear questions, and cliché answers, about the meaning behind the hurt and pain. It impacts all of us—even if we aren't the ones grieving. It cuts to our soul because we come face to face with the *hurt*, on one side, and the *joy* and *celebration* on the other, mixing its bittersweet fragrance in the air and spreading it to all on the wind.

The seasonal anthem could be heard in the background: **"Glory to God in the highest, and on earth peace, good will toward men!"** But they both sat in silence. The words only made the sting of the loss more obvious—and painful. Neither of them had been through something like this before. They finally spoke: "I just don't understand. Why did he have to go?"

"I don't know."

"We knew it was coming—just not this fast. You always think you're prepared for them to leave, but when the time comes, you realize that you're not."

"Isn't there something we can do?"

"It's out of our hands now."

"I suppose you're right."

"I wish I wasn't."

"Do you think God planned all of this?"

"That's what they say."

"Then I guess God needed him more than us."

"I guess so."

"This sure will change the holidays."

The music stopped as suddenly as it began. They turned to look at the carolers. Instead they saw the faces of the audience.

A small group.

Cold and tired.

Dirty and smelly.

Hardly worth singing to at all.

But their faces. That look on their faces. Such awe. Such wonder. Such amazement.

They got it! Those shepherds really got it!!

And at once the two angels understood. It was all worth it now.

"For unto us a child is born..."

What does it mean to our faith when we are living in days that are so uncertain? What does it mean when our minds are filled with anxiety and our stomachs are filled with butterflies? What does it mean when we plead with God to make sense of it all?

What does it mean when we fear being homeless—like Abraham?

"Do not be afraid, Abram. I am your shield" (Gen. 15:1 NIV).

Immanuel - - - God with us!

What does it mean when we fear making a living—like Isaac?

"Do not be afraid, for I am with you" (Gen. 26:24 NIV).

Immanuel - - - God with us!

What does it mean when we fear for the safety of our family—like Jacob did?

"Do not be afraid to go to Egypt; I will go down with you" (Gen. 46:3-4 NIV).

Immanuel - - - God with us!

What does it mean when we fear for our own safety—as did the disciples?

"Do not be afraid; I am here!" (John 6:20 NIV).

Immanuel - - - God with us!

What does it mean when there is a change in national leadership—like Joshua?

"Do not be afraid for the LORD your God will be with you" (Joshua 1:9 NIV).

Immanuel - - - God with us!

What does it mean when the miraculous happens—like angels talking to shepherds?

"Do not be afraid...a Savior is born to you" (Luke 2:10 NIV).

Immanuel - - - God with us!

What does it mean when a young girl faces the possibility of ridicule, exposure, shame, and death—like Mary?

"Do not be afraid; you have found favor with God" (Luke 1:30 NIV).

Immanuel - - - God with us!

Yes, there is fear in this world. Yes, we are facing times/things that are uncertain.

Yes, yes, yes, yes...the list goes on.

But from the beginning His message has been clear...certain...unaltered... personal.

It is the eternal Christmas message:

Immanuel - - - God with us!

In one of his letters to fellow believers the apostle Peter wrote: "So I will always remind you of these things, even though you know them and are firmly established in the truth you now have. I think it is right to refresh your memory" (2 Peter 1:12-13 NIV).

We've heard the story many, many times. The songs are all familiar and the words roll off our tongues with ease. The decorations around the house, on the tree, in the yard, all remind us of the **"Reason for the Season."** It is familiar—and so we forget to listen with a new, fresh, interested, absorbed, can't-wait-to-know anticipation.

The shorter, paraphrased version of Peter's words from above sound something like this:

"I've already told you this; but I'm telling you again!"

"For to us a child is born, to us a son is given, and the government will be on his shoulders. And he will be called Wonderful Counselor, Mighty God, Everlasting Father, Prince of Peace" (Isaiah 9:6 NIV).

"In the sixth month, God sent the angel Gabriel to Nazareth, a town in Galilee, to a virgin pledged to be married to a man named Joseph, a descendant of David. The virgin's name was Mary. The angel went to her and said, 'Greetings, you who are highly favored! The Lord is with you.'

"Mary was greatly troubled at his words and wondered what kind of greeting this might be. But the angel said to her, 'Do not be afraid, Mary, you have found favor with God. You will be with child and give birth to a son, and you are to give him the name Jesus. He will be great and will be called the Son of the Most High. The Lord God will give him the throne of his father David, and he will reign over the house of Jacob forever; his kingdom will never end'" (Luke 1:26-33 NIV).

"So Joseph also went up from the town of Nazareth in Galilee to Judea, to Bethlehem the town of David, because he belonged to the house and line of David. He went there to register with Mary, who was pledged to be married to him and was expecting a child. While they were there, the time came for the baby to be born, and she gave birth to her firstborn, a son. She wrapped him in cloths and placed him in a manger, because there was no room for them in the inn" (Luke 2:4-7 NIV).

"All this took place to fulfill what the Lord had said through the prophet: 'The virgin will be with child and will give birth to a son, and they will call him Immanuel' – which means, 'God with us'" (Matt. 1:22-23 NIV).

Yes, you already know this story - - - - *but I'm telling you again!*

"**Come**. Now Is the Time to **Worship**"—anytime we hear His gentle whisper or feel the tender touch of His presence.

When is the best time to worship? A chorus reminds us to "Come. *Now* Is the Time to Worship." Anytime we hear His gentle whisper or feel the tender touch of His presence it is time to worship. Some of my most precious worship experiences have come when I least expected them—at times when "worship" was not necessarily the "order of service" in the Sunday bulletin.

Previously I shared with you some of my prayerwalking experiences in Zimbabwe. A couple of days later we prayerwalked an area of the city where there was no church. We had unusual encounters with several individuals, all of which affirmed the need for a Christian witness there. As our small prayerwalking group sang, prayed and rejoiced in the Lord I realized I had never before worshipped with believers who expressed their faith with so much exuberance. Standing in a circle, clapping, singing and dancing, one by one the believers moved to the center of the circle to lead in the worship experience. I guess we would say that person was "bringing the special music"! In just a few weeks we began receiving news that the small group of believers was growing, and had become a large gathering of worshipers. Eighteen months later I had the joy of returning to that same church, once again worshiping with those believers. Imagine my surprise when, just before the morning's message, Pastor Reuben announced, "We are so happy to have Sister Judy back with us today. She is going to come now and dance for us!" My first thought? "Oh, if my daddy could see me now!" I left a part of my heart in that African country all those years ago, and my worship experiences have never been the same since.

I've been enjoying the rain. I mean, really, really enjoying the rain. To use a McDonald's phrase…I'm lovin' it! Why? Because I was supposed to mow the yard last Saturday. The task was already way past due so Saturday was the day—one of those "now or never" type of tasks.

It rained Saturday. *Well, what was I supposed to do?* I read a book, took at nap, played some cards, enjoyed the kids. After all, we could mow Sunday afternoon.

It rained Sunday. *Well, what was I supposed to do?* I watched the Cowboys, took a nap, read a book, played with the kids. After all, we could mow on Monday.

It rained Monday. *Well, what was I supposed…*ok, you get the picture.

Because of all this rain, our grass is growing rather quickly. What looked like an East Texas over-grown yard on Saturday has become an Amazon rainforest today! But even with the accelerated growth of the grass, I still felt justified for not being able to mow it. Nobody mows when the yard is wet, right?

It didn't rain Tuesday (at least at our house) and the ground was drying out a little. *Well, what was I supposed to do?* I took a nap, read a book, played with the kids.

It's been pretty easy for me to overlook the yard and come up with excuses for not mowing. It will eventually get done—it just isn't my first priority. After all…it's only grass!

But Scripture says the same about us. Look at Psalm 103, verse 15 & 16. **"As for man, his days are like grass, he flourishes like a flower of the field; the wind blows over it and it is gone, and its place remembers it no more"** (NIV).

I am so glad that God doesn't view us through the same lenses I use for my yard. I ignore it, put it off, come up with excuses to not pay attention to it, and then mow it down while I grumble and complain. Grass has no place of honor in my world.

But He chose a different focus.

He *fertilizes* us,
　　waters us,
　　　trims us,
　　　　weeds us,
　　　　　celebrates us.

He even took our place under the mower.

Well, what was I supposed to do? I thanked Him for grass!

Whoever coined the phrase *"it's a jungle out there"* was probably looking at my yard! After a week of vacation, and then a week of late afternoon rain, we were finally able to pull out the mower and attempt to tame this wilderness. And let me tell you…grass can *really grow* in two weeks when you're living in East Texas!

So, with this huge task in front of us, I decided the best approach was to face it like Moses. After all, he parted the Red Sea, turned the Nile River red with blood, and had frogs, gnats, and locusts descend upon Egypt. If there is someone to imitate it seems that Moses would be that person. My problem is that I started several chapters too soon. What I mean is this: God reveals Himself through Moses, with all of these signs mentioned above (and more), in the book of Exodus, chapters 7 through 14. I got stuck in Exodus 4. I took one look at that tall, tall grass and responded (just like Moses in 4:13), "O Lord, please send someone else to do it."

But as my son and I were out there sweating away…toiling under the hot sun…wasting away to nothing…sacrificing ourselves for the good of the neighborhood—me and my Moses attitude heard something that didn't seem to fit.

My son (who, by the way, didn't argue about joining me in the yard) was pushing the lawn-mower and **singing**!! Loud enough that I could hear him over the lawn-mower and the weed-eater. And he wasn't paying attention to anything, or anyone, around him except for the One he was singing to. And I felt like one of those weeds in the yard; it was very convicting.

How wonderful it is to know that God loves us so much that He won't allow us to dwell in our pity-parties. He uses the things, or people, around us to draw our attention back to Him.

"O LORD, our Lord, how majestic is Your name in all the earth!
    You have set Your glory above the heavens.
    From the lips of children and infants You have ordained praise"
    (Psalm 8:1-2 NIV).

Music touches the heart in ways that often take us off guard. A certain song may bring back pleasant memories from childhood, or that special relationship, those high-school years, even a wonderful period of peace in our lives.

Music is so very powerful when we are going through crisis. Most people can tell you the songs that were played or sung at a meaningful funeral or at the loss of someone deeply treasured. We connect the songs with the person, the event, and the emotions of the loss. And because of that connection, the songs mean more to us.

Music has always been a part of our faith. It lifts us up above and beyond the world of trouble that we are experiencing and sets us before the throne of God. We sing to praise, worship, pray, cry, express fear or gratitude, and all the other aspects of our relationship with God.

Sometimes it is the melody–upbeat and cheerful in one instance or slow and mournful in another–that sticks in our mind and buries the song deep in our heart. Other times it is the words–seemingly written just for us and our situation–that speak the truth of our joy or pain. Then, you combine the two and it feels as if your soul wants to leap out of your body because the music, words and notes, say what you have never been able to put into voice.

As far as hymns go, one that has not been around very long speaks volumes in combining all of the expressions mentioned above–joy and memories (God's ever-faithful presence and the fullness He brings to our lives), pain and loss (some days are scary and hard to face because we feel so very, very alone), faith and comfort (He makes it worthwhile even when the circumstances are rotten). The song assures us that "Because He Lives," we can face our tomorrows without fear, knowing that "He holds the future, and life is worth the living just because He lives."

You may remember the horrible shooting that took place at a church filled with teenagers in the Fort Worth area several years ago. We were shocked when the news came on the television, but even more shocked to see the face of one of our college classmates as he spoke of the unknowns taking place inside the building. His daughter was in there. He was scared.

We paid special attention to the news, both on the television and from our Alma Mater, for the next few days, hoping to catch a word about David's daughter. The news finally came from the school. She was one of those who had been shot and did not survive. Her parents were filled with grief but gave praise to God for His full understanding of an event that was too big for them to understand.

As we listened for the news about our friend's daughter, we heard other stories coming from the chaos. One was from a man whose wife was in the entry-way when the shooter came in. As he began firing, she turned to run down a hallway. She tripped, scared that the shooter was right behind her, got up to continue running, and tripped again. She got to her feet a second time and made it to safety. Without understanding why she was spared and others were not, her husband was hit hard by the last line of the second verse of a song that they sang in church. It goes something like this:

When I fall down You pick me up, when I am dry You fill my cup,
You are my All in all.

72

He saw this in powerful reality with his wife. He said that he was now unable to sing this particular song because he was so overcome with emotion–thankfulness and praise. God jumped right off the song-sheet and into their crisis.

Many old, familiar songs have the potential to overwhelm us with the same emotion–thankfulness and praise. We are standing in the middle of God jumping off the song-sheet and into the crisis of a very needy world. As you listen to the music, as you sing the songs–hear them brand new and let the message of the words carry your overwhelmed hearts to heaven.

Joy to the World, the Lord is Come
O Little Town of Bethlehem
Sweet Little Jesus Boy
O Come All Ye Faithful
Silent Night

He has picked us up from our fallen place. He has saved us from eternal separation from Him. He has jumped off the page and out of the manger.

"I will sing to the Lord, for He has been good to me" (Psalm 13:6 NIV).

```
4 7 8     6 2 9     3 1 5
6 2 9     5 3 1     4 7 8
3 1 5     4 7 8     6 2 9

2 8 7     9 6 5     1 4 3
9 4 3     1 8 2     7 5 6
1 5 6     7 4 3     9 8 2

5 6 1     2 9 4     8 3 7
8 9 4     3 5 7     2 6 1
7 3 2     8 1 6     5 9 4
```

I'm sure you have either heard of, or played, the game/puzzle Sudoku. The object is to fill in the blank squares in such a way that each of the numbers 1 to 9 appears exactly once in each row, column, and block, as you can see in the example above. My wife *loves* this game.

She has moved up in difficulty until she is now playing the hardest ones we can find. There are all kinds of methods and techniques to completing these puzzles, but the rules remain the same—numbers 1 to 9 appear only once in each row, column, and block.

Recently our youngest son came in while my wife and I were both doing Sudoku puzzles. (I was doing the EASY version!) He asked a few questions about what we were doing and then watched for a while. After a few minutes he said, "Who comes <u>UP</u> with these things!?"

Great question—on two levels! 1) Who has the time and creativity to create these puzzles and 2) there MUST be **someone** who makes them. You don't just throw a bunch of squares and numbers together and come out with a puzzle that has (remember the rules?) <u>1 to 9 **exactly once** in each row, column, and block</u>!!!

By now you are probably saying, "Duh, Perry. That's a no-brainer. Of course someone makes up these puzzles. No one would doubt that." And yet, all over this wonderful, amazing, creatively beautiful, beyond description world we live in where no two mountains, rivers, zebras, clouds, snowflakes, or people are the same, we still have trouble seeing that there is <u>**Someone**</u> behind it all.

We don't doubt the rules that are stated for the puzzle. Why is it that we doubt the rules stated for creation?

In the beginning God created the heavens and the earth.
And God said, "Let there be…and there was…(Gen. 1)

Don't be afraid to be the unique individual that you are in the **body of Christ**, with your special blend of talents, abilities, designs, and directions. That is how God planned it.

*F*or the body does not consist of one member but of many. Now you are the body of Christ and individually members of it"* (1 Cor. 12:14,27 HCSB). I can't help but think that Paul had fun when he was writing these words. In a humorous way he emphasized the significance of every body part, large or small, impressive or down-right ugly! Anyone who has ever had a broken toe or even a tiny paper cut knows just how much that small piece of bone and flesh can affect the entire body.

And what, you might be wondering, does being functioning members of the body of Christ have to do with "Or Now Is Fine"? Consider these thoughts:
* Many of Christ's assignments for us are specific to a time or situation, therefore our function as a body part varies. At one time He may need you to be His hands, touching a person who is in pain. Another time you may be the feet, carrying the Good News to the "uttermost parts of the earth." Perhaps at one time He needs you to be the lungs, bringing fresh air into the body, and another time expelling used air, detecting and removing unhealthy elements that would harm the body. Then sometimes you are simply a split, ragged fingernail protecting a vulnerable pinky. We can spend our time bemoaning the fact that we aren't an essential internal organ, or we can choose to do, with a joyful heart, "whatever turns up, grab it and do it. And heartily! This is your last and only chance at it, For there's neither work to do nor thoughts to think In the company of the dead, where you're most certainly headed" (Eccl. 9:10 TMB).

* You are not the only body part, you know. Have you affirmed others who function alongside you? What about the *ear* who listens to your heartaches and helps you carry them? What about the *shoulder* that lifts the other side of your burden, making it lighter to bear? Suppose that *you* are the aforementioned vulnerable pinky we just mentioned; have you thanked the *fingernail* that protects you?

* When do we assume our roles as fully functioning, well-equipped members of the Body of Christ? I think you have already guessed the answer. Yes, today is the day to begin serving Him. Waiting for "big" opportunities, more training, better options, the right time—all may come some day, but what He wants from each of us is to follow and obey Him right now, today. It may be offering someone a smile or kind word; it may be lending a sympathetic ear; it may be a gentle touch. Whatever assignment He has for you today—Now Is Fine to be His body, and together we can move, walk—and perhaps even dance—with Him.

Compared to me, my daughter lives life at full-throttle. What I think takes tremendous energy—well, that's the norm for her. She is never ready for bed when everyone else is tired and she is always awake before anyone else in the house. She loves eating at church where she can pile food on her plate, but then just take a bite or two of each thing and push the rest of the food over to daddy.

The most obvious call to "storm the gates" of life is in her candy choices. I like _Peanut M&M's_—she likes **Sour Skittles**. I like _Life-Savers_—she likes **War Heads**. I like _Butterfinger_—she likes **Pop Rocks**. But the differences remind me of the disciples who followed Jesus. Let's take a look.

The disciples came to him and asked, "Why do you speak to the people in parables?" (Matt. 13:10 NIV) _Peanut M&M's_

Peter said to Jesus, "Lord, it is good for us to be here. If you wish, I will put up three shelters--one for you, one for Moses and one for Elijah." (Matt 17:4 NIV) **Sour Skittles**

His disciples answered, "Where could we get enough bread in this remote place to feed such a crowd?" (Matt. 15:33 NIV) _Butterfinger_

"Lord, if it's you," Peter replied, "tell me to come to you on the water." (Matt. 14:28 NIV) **Pop Rocks**

The disciples came to him privately, saying, "Tell us, when will these things happen? And what will be the sign that they are all about to be fulfilled? " (Mark 13:4 NIV). *Life Savers*

Then Thomas said to the rest of teh disciples, "Let's us also go, that we may die with him." (John 11:16 NIV) (spoken when Jesus was going to Bethany, where the Jewish leaders wanted to put him to death). **War Heads**

No matter how they responded, what they said, how they interpreted events, they were handpicked, chosen, secured in their relationship with Christ. And He had great big plans for them. So big that they literally transformed the world! Whether we are Almond Joy or Punch Straw believers, we also have been handpicked, chosen, secured into a relationship with Christ.

We always began our team meetings with some kind of fun "getting to know you" activity. On that particular day all 28 of us wrote some little-known fact about ourselves on a card then dropped the card in a basket. The basket was then passed around the group and cards drawn randomly. One by one statements were read aloud, and the group assignment was to guess who wrote it then move on to the next statement. All the statements had been read and identified, and everyone (except the writer!) was completely stymied. "All my adult life I have wanted to learn to skydive."

You see, the problem was that the only person left who had not been "guessed" was Conni. Quiet, dignified, poised, always perfectly groomed Conni! Surely not! Yes, she assured us, learning to skydive really was her secret passion!

I had the opportunity to work closely with Conni over the next few years, and she always remained that same quiet, dignified, poised, perfectly groomed woman I first met. But somehow, just knowing that inside her there was a skydiver waiting to be set free–to imagine her floating freely through the sky–made her all the more special to me.

From Oval Office to Open Skies

Former President George Bush, too, enjoyed skydiving. His first dive was in 1944 when as a 20-year-old Navy Lieutenant Bush parachuted from his disabled torpedo bomber. After that experience he promised himself that some day he would dive again–this time for fun. His second jump came at age 73 and the next on his 75th birthday. After that jump someone asked if he would do it again. "I would, but I might wait till I'm 80," he replied.

Sure enough, at age 80, he did it again! On Friday, June 11, 2004 Bush delivered a eulogy at a memorial service for Former President Ronald Reagan. Then on Sunday, with a crowd of thousands watching, he parachuted 13,000 feet over his presidential library.

I have known far too many people who live life in the bleachers instead of on the playing field, haven't you? They are the ones who have forgotten that it's okay to laugh and play, to be silly and impractical and spontaneous, to live life with all the gusto they can summon. Perhaps they are not waiting until they grow up; perhaps they "grew up" so long ago they need to be a child again.

An Unexpected Career

When she was 67 Anna Mary's husband Thomas died. For awhile she focused on creating embroidery pictures, but when her arthritis made those projects too difficult, Anna Mary picked up a paint brush. The rest of the story is history. You might recognize Anna Mary by her husband Thomas's last name–Moses. Yes, when she died at age 101 Grandma Moses had produced some 2,000 paintings, most of them on Masonite board.

She shared her love of life with others through her paintbrush. At her 100th birthday party, it is said that Grandma Moses danced a jig. Just before her next birthday she had to be placed in a nursing home, which she despised because she was not allowed to paint. She even hid the doctor's stethoscope, promising to give it back if she could go home! An elementary student writing about the life of this remarkable woman said, "We are lucky she started painting." As I read this I wondered, "What would the world have been like if Grandma Moses had never started painting? If all those people who have made contributions to our lives had waited for a 'better day' to start?" We are indeed "lucky" and blessed that so many people have taken that first step–even if it was stepping out an open airplane door–and made the world a richer place for us all.

I recently saw this caption on a little league player's tee-shirt: "You'll never make it to second base if you stay on first." Henry David Thoreau wrote that "most men lead lives of quiet desperation and go to the grave with the song still in them." How sad it is to come to the end of this wonderful adventure of life never having sung the song, painted the picture, run the marathon (or to second base), or shared the smile that was inside.

? Who or what is inside you wanting to be set free? Is today the day you should pick up the paint brush or strap on the parachute?

SEND	To.....	Mom@ABQ.com
	From...	Perry@Tyler.com
	Subject:	Another Point of View

Remember when Joel was three years old and he was singing that praise song from church—"He is exalted, the King is exalted on high" . . . but Joel was singing, "He is exhausted, the King is exhausted on high"? We were reading your stories about George Bush and Grandma Moses and it brought to mind those times when we really DO want to do something but we are too exhausted, or the finances aren't there, or our health changes and it isn't physically possible anymore. You know, all those times that we WOULD jump in (if we could) but we can't. And the cool part is . . . it doesn't take God by surprise! He isn't burdened that we never made that trip to see the New England autumn, or hike the Rockies, become a scrap-booker, or even write a book (hmm). Yes, we need to dive in and do them "with gusto," if possible—but we also need to NOT beat ourselves up if we aren't able. It might be God's Stop! or His Wait! because we know . . . He is NEVER exhausted!!

My annual physical...went in fine; came out sick. My doctor was concerned about my weight. I told her that I think it is because I drink too much of a certain carbonated soft drink that comes in a red can. She jerked her head around to look at me, eyes wide open in shock, and emphatically said, "No, no, no, NO! You can't drink that...ever! You can't drink sweet tea. You can't drink *anything* with that much sugar!"

So I quit. Cold turkey. Not one more classic, full-sugared soft drink since that visit. And I was PROUD! I don't mean "proud" with small letters and a humble spirit. I mean PROUD!! Shout it from the rooftops, throw a party, and let the whole world know PROUD. The kind of proud you can only get from succeeding in a task that you personally deem to be impossible. Yep, _that_ kind of proud.

So on my next visit, six months later, I pointed out the fact that I had not had a Coke since my last office visit. I expected a free lollipop (sugar free, of course) or something for my wonderful work. Her response? "And **still** you weigh the same."

You see, I hadn't changed much of anything else. I hadn't started exercising. I hadn't changed my eating habits. (After all, who else is going to finish off the rest of the pizza, chips and cookies if I don't? It's a shame for them to go to waist...oops, that should be waste.) I quit the soft drinks—but I didn't change the way I think.

Romans 12:2 tells us we are to be transformed by the renewing of our minds. That's not, "Woo Hoo!! I believe! That's good enough; I'll stop there!"

It's more along the lines of, "I believe. So now I will let my believing change the way I think; and my thinking change the way I act; and my actions change the way I feel."

We are exercising now. And being more mindful of what we eat, how much, and what time (I sure did love those late night snacks). And it is becoming easier. I have passed up three desserts this week. It wasn't because I was depriving myself; I just didn't want them. HUGE change from last summer. And when I see the doctor again I won't be waiting for a pat on the back for my hard work. I'll keep working no matter what the response...because I want to.

Our faith calls us to think differently, to see things from God's perspective, so that our actions change *for real*. Not just laying some things aside yet finding out we "still weigh the same." Instead, to change the way we view the world and interact with it, because we want to, for the health of *His* body.

— — — — — — — — — — — — — — —

Jaydee was the center of our family focus: she was eight years old on that day. She had lived in our home for all of those years, minus 5 months. She had lived in our hearts much longer.

It was in college, way back when my wife and I were "just friends," that we shared our mutual dreams of someday adopting a child. Who knew that we would one day marry?! The plan wasn't the focus of our lives as God blessed us with three boys. But I remember well the day that I walked into the kitchen after work and saw Kelley sitting at the table. As she shared what God was doing in her life, she said, "We have a child out there," to which I immediately answered, "Let's go get her."

That started a wonderful journey that God brought to fruition with Kim Joo Ran—today known as Jaydee Anne. She hadn't been born yet when we charged forward with all the paperwork and process of adoption that cemented our love for her with the same passion that we feel for our boys. The "trip of a lifetime" across the ocean to pick her up seems so small compared to the thousands of oceans I would cross to be with that girl: to keep her safe; to show her this daddy's love; to provide for her needs; to let her know she is wanted and she has a home. That girl is MINE, folks. Don't forget it.

Listen to what God is saying, about *you*, from His Word–paraphrased by Eugene Peterson: "Long before He laid down earth's foundations, He had us in mind, had settled on us as the focus of His love, to be made whole and holy by His love. Long, long ago **He decided to adopt us into His family** through Jesus Christ" (Eph. 1:4-5a TMB).

He made a trip of a lifetime, across the galaxies of His creation, to take on flesh–to trade immortality for mortality; unlimited for limited; unbounded for bound; timeless for time-constrained–and took on the biggest fight of all creation at the cross to buy our salvation, to keep us safe, to show His Daddy's love for us, to provide for our needs, to let us know that we are wanted and that we have a home. And to say to us, "You are MINE, folks. Don't forget it."

I turned on the television.
  I saw a beautiful sanctuary,
    And heard a hundred voice choir sing a beautiful anthem,
      Accompanied by an orchestra.
  Then a soloist with an outstanding voice
    Sang a special of professional quality.
  The minister who spoke was eloquent and well-prepared,
    His voice and looks were pleasant,
      His message clear and understandable.
  And his sermon outline was a Power Point!
Then I went to church.
  The building was cold, and hadn't been cleaned.
    The pews were hard; the hymnals torn.
      Half the choir was off key,
        The other half looked like they were at a funeral.
  The organ growled; the piano was out of tune.
    The song leader didn't show up...would anyone volunteer?
      And if the sermon had an outline,
        I never did figure it out!
But the television never hugged me. Mary did.
  The TV minister never shook my hand. Bro. George did.
    No one in the hundred voice choir smiled at me. Karen did.
I turned off the television and never saw those people again.
  I left the church on Sunday,
    But I enjoyed my church family all week.
      The television preacher never prayed for me by name.

My pastor did.
Yes, I enjoy the great music
  And orchestra
    And professional singers
      And good sermons
        And well-planned services.
But even more, I enjoy the hugs
  And handshakes
    And smiles
      And prayers
        And fellowship.
I may not enjoy the song sung off key,
  But I love the people who are singing.
The sermon may be dull and hard to understand
  But the minister's love for his people is obvious.
    He may not be a preacher of renown–
      But he is a pastor worthy of note to me!
You chose a manger in a barn
  Over an ivory cradle!
Thank You, Lord, for Little Churches
  And Humble Mangers.

The scenery is the same every Saturday morning; a black and white ball, yellow and blue athletic uniforms, and dozens of young children running after that ball trying to score a goal. Yep, we are in the middle of soccer season.

I've been coaching for several years now and it never ceases to amaze me–with younger kids, no matter how much time you spend practicing other options, they just naturally want to play what is affectionately known as "bunch ball." They *all* chase the ball–no matter where it is on the field. Not some of them. Not just the fastest ones. Not the most aggressive. Not the ones who have never played before. ALL!! They chase after that ball and huddle around it to the point that they can't kick it (too many feet in the mix) and they can't pass it. (Who would they pass to? There isn't anyone separated from the bunch!) But you can't deny the fact that each kid is giving their all to get the work done for their team.

The scenery is the same every Sunday morning; a black jacket and white shirt, yellow tie and blue dress, and dozens of faithful church attendees running around the church trying to "score the goal" of the Christian life. Yes, even in church we have "bunch ball" mentality—giving our all to get the work done for our team.

In the book of First Corinthians, Paul says, "I planted the seed, Apollos watered it, but God made it grow." He was encouraging the people to not play bunch ball around the name of the Paul team or the Apollos team. He was saying, "Hey, folks. Everyone has a task, and everyone needs to do his/her task, so that together we can do what God has called us to do—and let God do what only God can do!"

We need the team. We need someone at the goal to block the shots. We need defenders who will create a barrier to the opposing team's advance. We need the mid-fielders who will switch focus quickly between defense and offense. We need the forwards who will make every attempt to score for our team. We need them all, in their place, doing their task, and trusting others to do their part, so that together the team can work efficiently. But it doesn't come naturally.

We must learn to listen to The Coach, follow His lead, do the task He has assigned (called) us to do, let others on the team do what they are assigned (called) to do, and trust that He can see a bigger picture than what we see out on the field.

"I blocked, Apollos passed, but God called the plays!"

― ― ― ― ― ― ― ― ― ― ― ― ―

Are you growing up or growing old? They are two sides of the same coin, you know. The only difference is that growing *up* makes plans for the future; growing old foresees the time when there is no future. Have you noticed that some young people are old, while others have lived many years yet have never grown old? I heard someone say recently that aging is inevitable; growing old is optional.

My grandmother thought it was optional. Though Mom was 98 when she died, I don't think she knew till the last six months that she was old. When she was 82 she showed me a pattern for a beautiful velvet quilt. "I think I'll make one of those when I am old," she told me. She was serious!

On her 95th birthday several of her family gathered for a birthday party. After the others left she gave me a beautiful, intricate 2' by 2' sample quilt square she had recently completed. I was amazed at the detail and precision; it was truly a work of art. Many hours of labor had gone into just this one block. "You might as well have this," she sighed. "I don't think I'll ever get a quilt like this made."

At 96 her doctor suggested that she might want to start using a walking cane as she worked in the small garden in front of her retirement apartment. "I don't want to use this thing. People will think I'm old," she complained.

One of my friends says that we will all grow old if we live long enough! Growing older does not mean that we must give up our dreams or our joy in living. Growing older can mean growing wiser and richer in the areas of life that are really important; it can be the real celebration of a life lived well. Realizing that we are indeed growing older should give us an attitude of gratitude for *today*, remembering that every day is a gift from God, a day when we can become more like the Master.

A King, a Prophet and a Preacher

About the age of 20, Solomon assumed the weighty responsibility of a kingdom. To many, I am sure, he seemed far too young to take on such heavy duties. Shortly into his reign God appeared to him in a dream, saying, "What can I give you? Ask" (1 Kings 3:5 TMB).

If, at age 20, you were given a kingdom to rule, what would you ask for? Immediately after becoming king Solomon encountered a situation requiring insight. Recognizing that he was "too young for this, a mere child!" he asked for the wisdom. This might have been one of those "Or Now Is Fine" moments! God was pleased with Solomon's request and granted his wish, giving him "the ability to lead and govern well" and a "wise and mature heart."

Another Old Testament young man, however, wanted to use his youth as an excuse for not doing *right then* what God wanted him to do. This young man, Jeremiah, heard God say, "Before you were even born I chose you to be a prophet."

Jeremiah replied, "Okay, Lord, when I grow up I'll be a prophet. But right now I'm just a kid. Why, I wouldn't have any idea what to say to all those *adult* people. And they wouldn't listen to *me*."

How did God answer him? "You're right, Jeremiah. We'll give you a few years to study theology, practice public speaking at the forum, and get established financially. Then we'll talk about this again." Hardly! Instead God said, "Look, I've put my words in your mouth. I have given you this responsibility, and I'm going to be with you. Really, I'm the One doing it and you're just my tool. Now let's get on with the assignment."

Many years later Paul mentored another young man who apparently had some of the same issues to deal with in his life. I wonder if some of Timothy's congregation might not have said or at least thought, "When he matures and takes a few leadership courses, possibly he'll be a good leader."

"He's not much to listen to now, but hopefully, with practice, someday he'll get better." Perhaps Timothy himself had those same or similar thoughts. "When I grow up I'll be a great preacher like Paul" or maybe even "When I grow up I'll be a physician and writer like Luke."

Paul told Timothy he was not to "let anyone put you down because you're young. Teach believers with your life: by word, by demeanor, by love, by faith, by integrity. Stay at your post reading Scripture, giving counsel, teaching. And that special gift of ministry you were given when the leaders of the church laid hands on you and prayed—keep that dusted off and in use. Cultivate these things. Immerse yourself in them. The people will all see you mature right before their eyes!" (1 Tim. 4:12-15 TMB).

Young people say "when I grow up;" those who recognize the brevity of life begin thinking about "when I grow old." Retirement for many is the proverbial carrot hanging in front of the mule, dutifully pulling the plow. Frank said that all his life he anxiously waited for the time when he could afford to go into a restaurant, order whatever he wanted, and never look at the cost. "Now," he sighed, "I have reached that place in life and the doctor won't let me have any of it!"

Paul wrote that "we should no longer be children...but grow up in all things into Him" (Eph 4:14-15 NKJV). Bottom line, whether we are growing *up* or growing *old,* we can choose to live each day to its fullest–realizing this is our only opportunity to live this day. When asked their greatest fear people often say it is of growing old, forgetting that worry itself increases the aging process.

My friend Dan wrote an article about experiences he, Linda and their three young sons had while they were attending college and seminary. His summary statements are forever printed on my heart–probably because they are so true for so many of us. "We thought we were preparing for life. We didn't realize we were living it." I have few regrets in life, but as I reflect on the days of preparation, young children, financial struggles, parenting teenagers, etc. I wish I had concentrated more on the living of each day of life rather than the anticipation of days ahead.

Do you think you are too old?

Abraham was 75 when God commanded him to leave his home and go to a "new land."

Sarah was 90 when she gave birth to Isaac.

Moses was 80 when he received his greatest assignment.

Joshua was 80 when he led the children of Israel into their Promised Land.

Solomon was an old man when he wrote Ecclesiastes.

Dr. Seuss collected 27 rejections before publishing his first written and illustrated book.

Do you think you are too young?

What if Daniel, Shadrach, Meshach and Abednego had said,

"We are too young to take a stand before the king"?

What if Saul had said,

"I'm too young to hear the voice of God Himself"?

What if David had said,

"I'm too young to face the giant Goliath"?

What if Jesus had looked at the cross and said,

"I'm too young to die"?

Or Now Is Fine.

--- --- --- --- --- --- --- --- --- --- --- --- ---

It's pretty easy to look around the hospital where I work and see how we all work together for a common goal/purpose. Each person has his or her individual focus and abilities but it is in bringing them together that we are able to help, to the fullest, the families that enter our doors. There are nurses, respiratory therapists, physical therapists, administrators, folks in the business office, doctors, housekeepers, chaplains...and the list goes on and on.

We wouldn't think of having a hospital without all the "parts" that bring about the successful "whole." Take out any of those positions mentioned above, or any of the others that aren't mentioned and we just can't fulfill our purpose. It takes us all.

It is easy for us to see this with the hospital. I think we often overlook it with the church. But as obvious as the hospital appears to us, the church (the Body of Christ) appeared to Paul. Listen to his words in Philippians chapter 2:

"If you have any encouragement from being united with Christ, if any comfort from His love, if any fellowship with the Spirit, if any tenderness and compassion, then make my joy complete *by being like-minded, having the same love, being one in spirit and purpose.*"

Basically he is saying, "Hey folks, you're all different, with different gifts and abilities, different looks and preferences, different skills and strengths, different likes and dislikes, but you have a common purpose–namely, representing Christ as Messiah to fulfill His work. So do it!"

Let's not just *show* how the Church is supposed to look. Instead, let's really BE the Church!

As you already know, I send a weekly Faith Boost to the staff of the hospital where I work. My mom is on my email list and she stated that she can tell who wrote the devotion for that day just by reading the first few lines. I guess we all have a particular "style." Anyway, she then goes to the bottom of the page to see if she is right. She said that she <u>KNEW</u> I didn't write a recent one because the first sentence was, "*Over the past few months I have been restoring a 1946 garden tractor that I bought at a garage sale.*"

Her message made me laugh—because I knew that she was right. I'd **never** take on the task of restoring an old tractor!

And here's the cool thing about it—*I don't have to!!!* God never intended for me to find my own personal worth in restoring a 1946 garden tractor (by the way, that was my fellow chaplain Robert writing those words), or shopping at the Sears parts center (Robert—again), or being a "hoops fan" (Alan, another chaplain), or playing catch with a football while the snow was falling this past Easter weekend (also Alan). Those were topics for the devotions that they wrote. But here is what I **must** do. I must be faithful to what I have been called, created, designed, and positioned to do and be. And here is why:

"*The body is a unit, though it is made up of many parts; and though all its parts are many, they form one body. So it is with Christ. For we were all baptized by one Spirit into one body; now **you** are the body of Christ, and each one of you is a part of it*" (1 Cor. 12:27 NIV). Don't be afraid to be the specific individual that you are in the body of Christ, with your special blend of talents, abilities, designs, thoughts and directions. That is how God planned it. And He wants others to see your "unique-ness" in service to Him as soon as they read the first few lines of your life.

I wish you could have met my friend Selma. Born with cerebral palsy, she nonetheless attended college and earned her teaching degree. Inside her severely limited physical body dwelt a beautiful, sharp mind. After college she taught school, married David, also a CP victim, and together they gave birth to a healthy son.

When we knew Selma and David they were probably in their 60s. David, who was an engineer for the government, could drive but Selma of course could not. Did that stop her? Not at all! She was often seen speeding (yes, speeding!) along Aztec or Coal avenues on her three-wheel cart. I'm not sure what subjects she taught professionally, but she taught so many life lessons to so many people and in so many ways. It is my joy to share a few of the lessons Selma taught me.

Lesson 1: Nearly every Sunday morning she arrived at the church early so she could go into the prayer room and carry the activities of the day to the Lord. Her speech was so limited that often it was not easy for us to understand her. I'm so thankful that the Lord has no such hearing difficulties. I sometimes wonder if perhaps it is easier for Him to understand her prayers than many of mine with my own "speech impairments."

Lesson 2: Great sports fans, Selma and David never missed a New Year's Bowl or Super Bowl game if possible. One Sunday morning I overheard a conversation between Selma and Adele about the afternoon's game. "I want to watch the game, but I don't like Howard Cosell," Adele admitted. With laughter in her halting voice Selma replied, "You just have to take the good with the bad!"

Lesson 3: In a conversation about housework Selma told a group of us, "If I can't wash it in the dishwasher, I just throw it away!" Not bad advice about priorities.

Lesson 4: Because Selma could not write, Dalton gave her seminary extension tests orally, and David wrote the answers she gave him. After one question Selma responded, "No." David sighed heavily, shook his head and gave her a disgusted look. "Yes!" she quickly amended her answer! I guess the lesson is that if you make a mistake, correct it as quickly as possible, and do it with a laugh!

Lesson 5: There are more lessons I learned from this dear saint, but I end with number 5, because nothing compares to this bit of wisdom. Awkwardly taking our 13 year old Nita's hands in her own, Selma looked carefully, deeply into the teenager's eyes. "Honey, life is *just* what you make of it." Although every step was a struggle for Selma, I would say she truly embodied the attitude that "Now Is Fine" to move according to God's traffic light, wouldn't you?

? Aren't you thankful for all the Selma's God has placed in your life to teach you His lessons? Is there someone to whom you need to express your gratitude for lessons taught? If that is not possible, have you thanked God for wrapping so many of His good gifts to you in people?

To **Jesus' call,** "Come, follow Me" we might add,
"And now is fine!"

When Jesus called anyone to follow Him, we have no record of His ever indicating that "later" would be okay. The call was to obedience, and immediate obedience at that. The first disciples He chose were two brothers, working at their trade as fishermen. Jesus' call was simple: "Follow me" (Matt. 4:19 KJV). *The Message* says, "They didn't ask questions, but simply dropped their nets and followed. A short distance down the beach they came upon another pair of brothers, James and John, Zebedee's sons. These two were sitting in a boat with their father, Zebedee, mending their fishnets. Jesus made the same offer to them, and they were just as quick to follow, abandoning boat and father" (Matt 4:20-22 TMB).

Somehow I think if any of these would-be followers had said, "As soon as I…" Jesus might have interrupted, "Or Now Is Fine!" That was, in essence, what He later replied to the would-be follower who asked that he first be allowed to attend to details surrounding his father's death. The prospective disciple lost his opportunity, and so do we when we are hesitant to leave all, immediately upon hearing His call, and follow Him.

However, Christ's call in our lives can become more complicated than simply laying aside the "fishing nets" that involve us and falling in step behind the Teacher. (Personally, I would be more than happy to set aside fishing gear. Now quilting, that's a different story!) Because His call comes in many ways, and because we are each uniquely created, our responses to Him differ. I heard an evangelist tell of his growing up on a farm. He said that he would chop weeds from rows of cotton then fall on his knees at the end of the row and beg, "God, *please* call me to preach!" For many others the opposite seems to be true; some struggle for years with the decision to follow Him.

"Elizabeth" was an unusually attractive nursing student. For several months she had sensed that God was calling her to serve Him as a missionary in another country. Her heart's desire, though, was to have a family. She feared that if she "surrendered" to His call she would have to forfeit her dream. "Ed," also a student at the college of medicine, was fascinated with Elizabeth's charm. However, he had no doubts that God's call in his life was also to mission service. As attractive as Elizabeth was, he would not allow himself to be interested in her because he knew he would need a partner who was also committed to missions.

One Sunday evening during the invitation Elizabeth could no longer resist. "Okay, Lord, I'll go where you want me to go, even if it means giving up my dreams of having a family." Of course you know the rest of the story. God truly gave her the desires of her heart once she obeyed Him.

SEND		
	To.	Perry@Tyler.com
	From. . .	Mom@ABQ.com
	Subiect:	Your Call

Do you remember the night at camp when you first knew God had a special task for you? As you and I stood beneath the stars, surrounded by those tall pine trees, you asked, "But how can I know *what* God wants me to do?"

SEND		
	To.	Mom@ABQ.com
	From. . .	Perry@Tyler.com
	Subiect:	Re: Your Call

And do you remember what you told me? You compared it to driving at night. You said, "Our headlights only allow us to see so far into the darkness, but it is far enough for us to move into that light. And as we move forward, we see enough to continue the journey." In orientation I tell our nurses that one of the things I love about my job here at the hospital is that I get to "journey" with folks as they move through these crazy crisis life experiences that so often don't seem to make any sense and we can't see much of the path. I guess I'm still listening to your advice! Thank you for those words all those years ago!

Okay, imagine this: someone has written a book and it has become a best-seller. It has been read by millions and millions of people, in a variety of languages, all around the world. And you, yes YOU, happen to find your name and story included in this book.

Now, imagine this: the stories that include you are not very complimentary. One tells of how you were so scared that you ran away, leaving the hero of the book to stand all alone. If that's not bad enough, someone grabbed hold of your clothes and you were so intent on getting away that you ran away naked, leaving your clothes in their hand. Later, you abandoned some friends and a family member, in a foreign country, so you could go home. No reason given—you just headed home.

We have to use our imaginations to come up with these particular stories for our lives. Mark, also known as John Mark, lived them! Let's take a look:

"A young man (referring to Mark), wearing nothing but a linen garment, was following Jesus. When they seized him, he fled naked, leaving his garment behind" (Mark 14:51 NIV).

"From Paphos, Paul and his companions sailed to Perga in Pamphylia, where John (also known as Mark) left them to return to Jerusalem" (Acts 13:13 NIV).

"Some time later...Barnabas wanted to take John, also called Mark, with them, but Paul did not think it wise to take him, because he had deserted them in Pamphylia and had not continued with them in the work" (Acts 15:36-38 NIV).

We may have to use our imagination to see ourselves in Mark's stories, but we don't have to imagine to see our own faults and failures—all the times that we were too scared, too homesick, too uncertain, too weak, too young, too naked, too...whatever!

Finally, imagine this: redemption beyond anything we can comprehend; acceptance, even when we are miserable failures; grace, which brings growth and strength.

"My fellow prisoner Aristarchus sends you his greetings, as does Mark, the cousin of Barnabas" (Col. 4:10 NIV).

"Only Luke is with me. Get Mark and bring him with you, because he is helpful to me in my ministry" (2 Tim. 4:11 NIV).

"Epaphras, my fellow prisoner in Christ Jesus, sends you greetings. And so do Mark, Aristarchus, Demas, and Luke, my fellow workers" (Philemon 23-24 NIV).

"She who is in Babylon, chosen together with you, sends you her greetings, and so does my son Mark" (1 Peter 5:13 NIV).

OH, WAIT!! We don't have to imagine that. It's already been given to us, through Christ. Don't "imagine" that your failures define you. Choose to be defined by His grace instead!!

Non-stick coated pans—don't you love 'em? You throw whatever it is you want to cook in there and you have absolutely *no worries* about it sticking to the pan. Those eggs slide right out. Pork Chops? No problem. You name it—it won't stick.

And at first we are so cautious in our care for them. We don't place anything on top of them in the cabinet, we only use wooden or plastic utensils, and we take great care in their cleaning and drying. Until that day comes when something is just about to burn (because these pans seem to cook food faster than that old iron skillet) and in our haste we grab a fork and flip that meat over. And, wonder of all wonders, nothing bad happened to the pan! Food still doesn't stick. You can't see any damage at all!

So the next time a plastic, or wooden, utensil is placed just out of reach, we grab that metal fork. And there continues to be no damage. So it gets easier and easier to do—forget the guidelines, go with the quick fix, write your own rules. But the damage *is* being done. The no-stick coating is being **broken down**. And one day, seemingly without any warning, something sticks to the bottom of the pan. And it continues to get worse and worse until we end up throwing that pan out—or fussing every time we use it.

Something like that happened to us. We were rusty old iron pans and God came in with His own plan—Jesus—and placed a no-stick coating around our hearts, making it possible for us to resist sin (through His power) so that it didn't "stick" to us. And it worked for a while. We were so in love with God that we wanted to serve Him at every turn. But one day...oh, that one day (do you remember the time?)...we allowed ourselves that one little sin. No one noticed. It didn't hurt anyone. It isn't even worth mentioning.

The next time was easier. And even easier after that, until we reached a place where that "pet sin" seemed like it was normal instead of disobedience. But the lining around that heart is being scratched and nicked with each continuing sin, until we reach a place where we become painfully aware our relationship with God has **broken down**.

Numbers 32:23 reminds us that our sin will find us out.

God's call to us is to be holy, because He is holy. It isn't something we can do on our own. We need His grace in order for us to resist sin and live holy and pure.

Trust His work and the miracle of a redeemed (no-stick) heart. The blessings far outweigh the convenience of grabbing that metal fork or spatula!

We had a wonderful summer! There was a vacation trip to see family, time spent in the coolness of the mountains, visits with friends. There were church camps for the kids. There was the "Bayou Bombardment" of fireworks down in southern Louisiana for July 4th. There were trips to water parks. There was homemade ice cream, and when that ran out, there was Andy's frozen custard. And lots (lots, lots, lots) of time in the swimming pool.

But my favorite thing of the entire summer was listening to the laughter of the kids as they shared "inside jokes" with each other. A word here, a raised eyebrow there, the swing of an imaginary sword, and they were rolling on the floor in hysterics.

It was such a blessing, you see, because our oldest son was home from college. Sure, we talked to him while he was away at school. We knew all about his schedule, his classes, the professors, the cafeteria, his roommate, his church, his test grades, etc., etc. We were actively involved in his life—whatever that means from 8½ hours away! But you don't share the same LIFE events when you aren't "dwelling" with each other. You may hear about the concert, but not the stain on the tux jacket. You may hear about the backed-up washing machine in the dorm, but not the shine of the car after it was washed. You may hear about the incredible desserts, but not the Freshman Fifteen!

The only way to share "inside jokes" is to LIVE with each other...to experience the day-to-day of life with each other...to dwell with one another. That is the making of an entire story—told in just one word or sound!

Don't you find that we do the same thing with God? We get so wrapped up in living life that we make Him a part of it...reading the Bible every once in a while, attending church when we can, praying when we remember to do so—but we miss out on the moment to moment "dwelling" with Him. We miss out on the God-sized inside jokes (so to speak) because we really haven't had enough time together.

"Let the word of Christ dwell in you richly" (Col. 3:16 NIV).

Lord, I'm available.
  Now—here's my plan.
    What? Oh, I see.

  Lord, I'm available.
    What would You think of *this* plan?
      What? Oh, I see.

    Lord, I'm available.
      What is Your plan?

It was a thrill beyond compare. NOTHING made my heart jump, or a smile come to my face, quicker than the combination of these three things: a western movie listed in the newspaper for the Late Show, mom saying it was okay to miss regular bed-time, and dad saying he would watch it with me. And if you wanted to go ahead and push me over the edge...mom making popcorn *just for me and dad*!!!! Those were the days!

After the movie was over I'd race to my room to get my pistols and holsters and we would have our own "fast draw" competitions. Being a father now, I look back and see it differently. I'm sure my dad was intentional about letting me out-draw him and hold on to my title of the "fastest gun in the west."

But my grandfather...HE was a *real* cowboy. He homesteaded in New Mexico, wore a gun strapped to his leg, raised cattle, fought rustlers, built windmills, killed rattlesnakes, and had his own cattle brand. He was John Wayne without the cameras!

His brand was the /OK. I think its meaning is bigger than red-hot iron, charred cattle flesh, and singed hair. I think my grandfather was borrowing **God's** brand. Take a look:

When we talk about a "/" ("slash" in brand terminology) we think about something negative. We chop celery, slice potatoes, and cut meat, but we don't "slash" anything! It is seen as violent and harsh. Much like the harshness we face in life–the slashing of our souls when we get fired from a job, can't control a child, care for a sick parent, lose a spouse, and hundreds of other ways that the world attempts to beat the tar out of us.

"In this world you will have trouble." Plain spoken words by Jesus found in John 16:33 (NIV). Pretty straight-forward and blunt...in this world you will have to bear the marks from a certain amount of slashing. But that is not the only mark on the brand.

The "/" is followed by "OK."

"In this world you will have trouble." Now the verse continues. "But take heart! I have overcome the world." Sure, the tough times come. There may be things you think you can't endure, can't live through...but take heart! After the "slash" there is a big "OK".

It's not all Polly-Anna, pie in the sky, when you wish upon a star, fantasy dreaming. It is a deep hope in the One who is intentional about being in control even while we feel we are spinning out of control. The final marks are made; we are branded by His fire. We belong to Him. And no rustler can erase His mark on our souls.

Now THAT truly is a thrill beyond compare!

Aren't words amazing? The same word can clarify and confuse, depending on the use and how it is heard. Take a look at the word *so*.

"*So*, how are you this morning?"

"It's time to say *so*-long to July."

"I loved her *so* much."

"I miss him *so*."

"*So*..."

"... *so*..."

"... *so*"

"*SO* what!!"

It is such a small word, yet it has 19 different definitions and is spoken hundreds of times each day in a variety of ways. So, why this interest in the word *so* this morning? I'm so glad you asked!

It is comforting to those who believe it.

It comes quickly to the mind of those who have memorized it.

It carries a promise that is unequaled.

It remains true whether we accept it or not.

"For God so loved the world that He gave His one and only Son, that whoever believes in Him shall not perish but have eternal life" (John 3:16 NIV).

Nineteen definitions for one word. Wow! But in the above context it means "to a great extent." God's love for the world was, and continues to be, deeper, wider, higher, and stronger than any love that had been expressed before.

Our hearts ache when we see others hurting. We see folks who have lost that special someone they love. Maybe it's us who are experiencing the loss. We want to hold their hand, hear their voice, see their smile just one more time. It hurts so much and we long for them, because we loved them.

And sometimes it seems as if the world just doesn't understand. How could they? Who can know how I feel at this painful moment?

"For God so loved..."

So, you fell down.

Was it for nothing?

Peter said, "I don't know Him."

Jesus knew Peter would do that.

He said, "When you have turned back,

Strengthen your brothers" (Luke 22:32 HCSB).

And after Peter had denied Jesus,

And He died,

And rose again,
    He told Peter,
        "Feed My sheep.
           Now you are ready.
             Feed My sheep.
                Strengthen your brothers."
So, you fell down.
  Was it for nothing?

Every October, around the hospitals I've worked in, they send out a memo asking folks what type of calendar they want to order for the next year. I always get the same type because I have learned to read it quickly and it has the space on it that I need for all the little notes I write. But this year, I have a new calendar. It is one of those calendars for organized people. I was hoping it would make me organized. So far, I just have a new calendar.

But there is part of this calendar that is intriguing to me. It has an entire section devoted to your "Personal Mission Statement." We all have one. This is about the way you look at life. It involves the things you hold as important and how you carry them out in everyday living. Not too hard, right? But try putting that on paper! (Especially if you aren't organized.)

Most of our views come from people that we look up to; people we respect. I learned some of life's greatest lessons from a giant of a man who is only 5'7". He taught me how to stand up for what is right. He taught me to be kind to others. He taught me to be thankful for what I have (still working on that one). And he taught me, by carrying it out in his own life, that it is ok for a man to cry. Sometimes it was teary eyes. At other times, a few tears would run down his cheeks. And then there were the times he would get so choked up he could hardly talk. I didn't always understand it as a child, but as an adult I see that my dad loves people so much that sometimes the only thing he CAN do is cry.

I have been with many families over the years at that moment when death comes to a loved one. Some cry openly, and I am thankful that they can. Some express other emotions, and I am thankful that they feel the freedom to do so. But there are times when they cry and apologize to me for their tears. Maybe they grew up in a family where "crying is not ok." Or maybe they were raised not to show any emotion in public. They might be embarrassed at the loss of control or that they appear weak. Whatever the reason, they apologize. And it causes me to think about a man who impacted my life with tears that ran down his face...or should I say His face. Remember the story? When Lazarus died, Jesus wept (see John 11:35).

96

I don't mean to be patronizing; I hope it never comes out that way. But when I hear an apology for tears, I usually say, "You must love them very much." I see tears, not as a sign of weakness, but as a very particular expression of strength, because it takes a strong person to love deeply. That is part of my "Personal Mission Statement." And I'm thankful to those who helped me develop it… thankful to my father and my Father.

The conversation started off with a normal guy question: "So, what do you do?" When I stated that I work at East Texas Medical Center he immediately cut me off saying, "We have one of your ambulances." He works at Discovery Science Place where ETMC has an ambulance on display.

I've been around hospitals for 17 years. I've seen, heard, dodged, pulled over for, waved at, and followed ambulances. Thankfully I have never yet had the opportunity to ride in one. But notice his words: "We have one of *your* ambulances." Here I am, the proud owner of a teal and white box with flashing lights on the top, just because I say I work for this organization.

Ok, ok. So I don't really own an ambulance. But I am identified as a part of the ETMC team because of the ID badge on my collar and the name on the bottom of my paystub.

The conversation started off with a normal guy question: "Surely you are not another of this man's disciples?"

He'd been around Jesus for three years. He'd seen the miracles, heard the teachings, dodged the religious leaders, pulled over for the sick, lame, blind, waved at the cheering crowds, and followed this teacher all over the countryside. Was he now in danger of being the proud owner of a rugged Roman cross of his own, just because he could say that he knew this man?

They searched for ways to clarify the connection – with a second question, "Surely you are not another of his disciples?" and a third, "Didn't I see you with him in the olive grove?" Although he claimed otherwise, Peter was finally identified as part of the team…when the rooster crowed. You can read about it in the 18th chapter of the Gospel of John.

I could have denied association with the hospital but my actions would give me away. This is where I spend my time in ministry and care. This is where I make my living. This is where I am known as a team member. This is where I work.

Are we as quickly and obviously known for our faith as we are identified with the places where we are employed? Does our ID badge, the one that says "Christian" (little-Christ), make a difference in how we conduct ourselves? Does the name on the bottom of our pay-stub, the one that bought our souls and is signed in blood-red, make a difference in how we live out our daily lives? Will we be identified from the first words…"Surely you are not another of this man's disciples?" YES! I am! Or will we be identified only when we hear the rooster crow?

I had breakfast with Jesus this morning!
He died...then He rose again.
  Miracles of Miracles!
    And *He* ate breakfast with *me* this morning!
      Even after I had denied Him.
Why would He ever want to see me again?
  With an eternal task before Him,
    Why would He spend time with *me*?
      Yet *He* had breakfast with *me* this morning!
We talked about the fish, friends, family.
  We laughed, and cried, and remembered.
    We talked of things ordinary,
      And things too profound to put into words
        As we ate breakfast together on the lake side.
Then He looked at me...me, who denied I knew Him.
  He didn't ask, "Why did you do it?"
    He didn't say, "You should not have done that."
      He didn't say, "I *told* you so."
        He didn't ask, "Are you sorry?"
        He simply looked at me and asked,
          "Do you love me?"
Now, I can understand His asking that.
  After all, I had denied Him.
    I had returned to my fishing nets.
      I thought for only a moment then assured Him,
        "Yes, Lord, I love You. You know I do."
        And He replied, "Tend to My lambs."
I really didn't understand, but then,
  He often said things I didn't really understand.
    So I went on eating my fish.
Then He looked at me again. And again He asked,
  "Do you truly love me?"
    There was something in His voice,
      A mixture of urgency, of longing, of tenderness.
      I tried not to sound impatient or disturbed

As I replied, "Lord, *You* know I love you."
I had told Him I was sorry. Did He not believe me?
And He replied tenderly, "Be a shepherd to My sheep."
And a few moments later (or was it several minutes?)
He looked into my very soul, and He asked,
As though He were asking for the first time,
"Do you love Me?"
I might have noticed the tear in His eye
Had I not been so hurt by His words.
Was He not listening?
Didn't He hear a word I had said?
I could not hide my emotions.
I answered, perhaps more loudly than I should have,
"*Lord,* You know all things.
"*You* know I love You."
Then my voice broke, and I whispered,
"*You* know I love You."
And as I wept, He said gently, firmly,
"Tend My little lambs."
I was still going through so much.
I didn't yet have His Spirit within me.
I was still wrestling with my own emotions.
My doubts, my guilt, my fears of the unknown.
But I *do* love Him.
At least as much as I am capable of at this moment.
And He accepted my imperfect love.
He didn't say, "When you love me as you should,
Tend My sheep."
He gave me an assignment, now.
And I recalled His words to me earlier…
Was it really such a short time ago?
"After you have fallen, strengthen your brothers."
Now I understand.
I fell.
I failed Him so miserably.
Yet *He* ate breakfast with *me* this morning.
He accepted my imperfect love.
He renewed my assignment to tend His lambs,
To strengthen them because of what I learned

About Him…about myself.

Thank You, Lord, Master, Friend,

For accepting my life as it is—imperfect, immature.

For giving me a work to do, in spite of my failures.

For eating breakfast with *me* this morning.

Unskilled labor—yep, that describes my carpenter ability to a tee! And apparently I am not alone in my "lack" of skills because 4,000 others volunteered…so many that I wasn't needed.

What am I talking about? *What was all of East Texas talking about?* EXTREME MAKEOVER: HOME EDITION!!!! They were building in the area, preparing to "move that bus" as another well-deserving family received a new home, graciously put together by neighbors, friends, and fellow East Texans. It's very exciting…but not original.

They borrowed the idea…you know, the idea of coming in and destroying the old in order to build the new. God has been doing this for ages!

"Therefore, if anyone is in Christ, he is a new creation; the old has gone, the new has come!" (2 Cor. 5:17 NIV).

I am thrilled that this family received a new home. But eventually this home will wear out too. One day this "new" home will just be another "old" home… again.

But God is doing a work that won't wear out in those who have placed their faith in Christ! It *can't* wear out! The "old" is GONE!! The "old" was destroyed; that nature is not the principal structure on the building lot of our lives. And constant remodeling is going on, by the Lord's hand, to keep the new structure "new." Now THAT is defined as <u>skilled</u> labor!

And that's not all. We will have a home/dwelling/body/nature that will live forever with Him in heaven. "This Old House," so to speak, can't survive in that holy environment.

But…we are a new creation!

EXTREME MAKEOVER: GOD EDITION!!!!!!!!!!

We have been to two (2) junior high track meets in the past week. One was long, the other was…longer! But we had such a great time cheering for our son, and for his teammates, as they competed in all of their events.

It was thrilling to see the burst of speed with which our son literally took over the pack on his very first race. We had never seen him run (he tends to not move quickly–ever!) and we sat there with our mouths open. It was fantastic!

It was hilarious to hear the family behind us cheering for their son. They must have brought ALL the kin-folks. This huge crowd was making a super amount of noise in support of their runner.

It was fun to hear the nick-name given to the relay team our son is on–The "J" Train. See, all of the boys on this relay have names that start with the letter "J". And *they move out!*

But there is something else that is wonderful to watch at these track meets. Remember, these are junior high runners and they are just starting to experience competitive sports, what they *want* to run, and what they are *able* to run. It would be easy for them to fall behind in a particular race and give up, throw out excuses such as "this just isn't MY best distance," or quit completely.

But instead...we see teammates and coaches, parents and classmates, siblings and opposing team coaches, and voices from all over cheering wildly and encouraging that final straggler who feels better equipped for the 100 meter rather than the 2400 meter. And we see these kids CROSS THE FINISH LINE!

It was tough.

They are finished, in more ways than one.

But they stayed with the race and completed it.

King Solomon, the Apostle Paul, and the writer of Hebrews must have attended some junior high track meets as well. Listen to what they have to say:

"I have seen something else under the sun: the race is not to the swift" (Eccl. 9:11 NIV).

"Do you not know that in a race all the runners run, but only one gets the prize? Run in such a way as to get the prize" (1 Cor. 9:24 NIV).

"Let us run with perseverance the race marked out for us" (Heb. 12:1 NIV).

"I have fought the good fight, I have finished the race, I have kept the faith" (2 Tim. 4:7 NIV).

Keep running! And know that "there is a great cloud of witnesses" cheering you on–no matter how hard the race!

SEND	To.	Perry@Tyler.com
	From. . .	Mom@ABQ.com
	Subject:	Your First Track Meet

Please forgive me, but I must include this! You just reminded me of the first track meet you attended. You were five; your cousin John was running the high hurdles. He was fast, but he came in second. Indignant, you put your hands on your hips and declared, "Well, if they'd just gotten those things out of his way John could have won!" So many times I have reflected on that experience. The hurdles defined the race; to remove them would defeat the intent. You reminded us earlier that in this life we *will have trouble*. There *are* hurdles on the track field. To run the race well, we must approach the obstacles with determination, keeping our eye on the finish line and putting our best efforts into the challenge at hand. Sometimes I want to sit down on the field and say, "I just can't make it over one more hurdle." I guess an alternative would be to keep running but try to go around the hurdles, but for sure I'd lose the race then! Anyway, thank you for reminding me to keep running, for cheering me on, and for the lessons you've taught me. I love you!

When is the best time to **share His love** with someone else? I'm sure you know the answer!

Whether skydiving, painting or telling someone what a difference Christ has made in our lives, it is easy to say I'll do that some other time.

"I don't know enough about the Bible."

"What if they ask a question that I can't answer?"

I think of the many parents I have heard say, "Timmy is asking questions about becoming a Christian. I need to take him to talk with our pastor." Mother and possibly Daddy were there when Timmy was born the first time. How sad if they miss the joy of guiding him to his second birth.

I must admit, I am a bit envious of people who have the gift of evangelism. As Jay and I were about to thank God for our lunch, the waitress arrived with our food. Jay reached for the young lady's hand and said, "We are just about to pray. Do you have anything we can pray about?"

Tears came in the waitress's eyes as she told us that her husband had recently lost his job and that afternoon had a job interview. Needless to say, tears came to our eyes also, and the prayer was a lot more than "Thank-you-God-for-the-food. Amen."

Several years ago I adopted my friend Verne's habit of closing a conversation with "Have a blessed day." The checker at Albertson's, the caller letting me know that Clothes Helping Kids is coming to my neighborhood, Sabrina calling to remind me of my doctor's appointment the next day…all get my usual "have a blessed day." Recently, though, as I left the check-out stand at Wal-Mart I smiled at the checker and said,

"God bless you." Surprised at my own response, for just a second I thought "Where did *that* come from?"

The checker reached out, took my hand and said, "Thank you. I needed that." I left feeling thankful that God chose to use my voice to speak His blessing to one of His children.

? When is the best time to share His love with someone else?
• When we know just the right thing to say? Or Now Is Fine.

? When do we express our gratitude to Him or confess an
• ungodly thought? Just before we fall asleep at night? "It is good to praise the LORD, to sing praise to Your name, Most High, to declare Your faithful love in the morning and Your faithfulness at night" (Psalms 92:1-2 HCSB). Or Now Is Fine.

? When do we pray for the person who asks for our prayers?
• When we have our quiet time in the morning? Do we say, "I'll be praying for you" then forget till we see the person next time? Oops! Or Now Is Fine.

"It was a dark and stormy night."

There he sits, up on top of his doghouse, typewriter at the ready. Charles Shultz had no idea what he was starting when he had Snoopy type that first line back on July 12, 1965.

Most people attribute the line to Snoopy instead of the original author (Edward Bulwer-Lytton back in 1830). Snoopy has revised his story over the years. Sometimes adding more, sometimes unable to write anything, sometimes bearing the brunt of criticism from Lucy. But still he writes. And history was made!

"It was a dark and stormy night.
Suddenly, a shot rang out!
A door slammed.
The maid screamed.
Suddenly, a pirate ship appeared on the horizon!"

Everything happened so fast! Who fired the shot? Why did the maid scream? Was anyone's momma going to fuss because a door was slammed? And what little boy wouldn't be drawn in by a pirate ship?! As a child, I always looked forward to those times when Snoopy would find himself at the typewriter.

As I grew, I began reading the Gospel of Mark with the same anticipation. I found myself, once again, running through the story...asking questions, feeling the adrenaline rush, and ready to fight the pirates (or storm).

"It was a dark and stormy night.
Immediately the disciples got in a boat!
The crowds were sent away.
The disciples screamed.
Immediately Jesus appeared, walking on the water!"

Where were the disciples going? Why was the crowd sent away? Is anyone going to fuss if the disciples sink this borrowed boat? And who wouldn't be amazed at Jesus <u>walking</u> on water?! Like Snoopy, Mark writes with a sense of urgency...*there's a story to be told, let's not waste time!*

Is there urgency in your story? Does it leap off the page, or tongue, begging to be shared?

"It was a dark and stormy night.
Suddenly I cried out to God!
The door of my heart flew open.
Immediately I found hope!"

The original design was elaborate; one-of-a-kind; bold; classy; God-ordained (at least that was MY impression). The final outcome showed only a lopsided igloo with a removable top. To say it resembled anything else would be a stretch. I called it a cookie jar. My 6th grade art teacher called it a "C minus."

I still love to mold things out of Play-Doh. It is part of the joy of being a parent. You can squish it, mash it, shape it, flatten it, and design it to your heart's content and no one says a thing because you are playing with your children. Maybe I'm trying to make up for those days long ago in art class when I was given a lump of clay and "encouraged" to make an original sculpture. Or maybe I just like to see how something turns out when I am the one pushing and prodding it to take shape. Whatever the reason, there is a certain joy that comes from touching that cold clay and knowing that whatever design or shape it takes...no one can do it just like you!

But it isn't always pleasant. Molding clay has a dirty, dusty smell. It is cold to touch and slimy when you add water. It is stiff and heavy and doesn't always look like you want it to look, even when you have invested a great deal of energy and time.

We find the same thing with the people who weave in and out of our lives every day, impacting us in ways often unimaginable. We touch their lives and *they* touch ours, offering pressure and direction that can only come from their particular touch. Sometimes it is pleasant. Sometimes it hurts. But if we allow for the change, it is always for the better.

The leper knew he was unclean. He had to warn folks when he was near so they could avoid him and his horrible illness. He hadn't been touched for a long time and his request didn't include touch, or even closeness. But he got down on his sore knees and cried out, "Lord, if you are willing, you can make me clean." There must have been electricity in that moment, like when you drag your feet across the carpet and then reach out and shock someone! Jesus reached out His hand and touched the man. "I am willing," He said. "Be clean!" (You can find the story in Matthew 8.)

He reached out to bad smelling, cold, slimy, stiff, heavy molding clay that had been designed into the shape of a broken and hurting man, and He **touched** him. And changed his life.

Your elaborate, one-of-a-kind, bold, classy, God-ordained touch may look like a sagging igloo to some folks. But to God it looks like an A+. And to the person you touch, it gives warmth and design.

Now is a good time to "reach out and touch!"

If you don't know the joy and wildness of moving in the rhythms of His grace, grab hold and hang on! Today could be the start of an **incredible relationship**! Believe me . . . Now Is Fine!

Thank you, Dear Reader, for taking this journey with us. Every path offers a fuller, deeper experience when it is shared. You have taken the time to hear our stories and we hope they have triggered memories and served as reminders of the times in your own life where you have known the unmistakable stirring of the Spirit. Those are times to cherish, to feast upon, to bask in...and then to share—so that others might experience the Hand of God moving in this day-to-day world.

Yes, it is a *miraculous* life—for only God can be credited with the creation of us as people. He planned us, formed us, breathed life into us, sustains us, redeems us, loves us, and holds our place with Him in eternity. Absolutely, no questions about it...a MIRACLE!

Yes, it is a mundane life—the sometimes boring, uneventful, sameness of everyday matters that flow from day to day, month to month, and year to year. To borrow the phrase from a childhood book, "nothing ever happens on my block." It might be difficult to find God in the water puddle under the kitchen sink, the flat tire in the driveway, the weeds overtaking the grass, and the "extra fee" for the school fieldtrip, especially when the money just isn't there this paycheck!

And in all of those times—the miraculous and the mundane—we find ourselves moving in His grace, for He promises, "I am with you always" (Matt. 28:20 NIV).

Most of you reading this book know that promise. Sometimes you've rested in that truth and sometimes you've questioned it. But you know it, because you know Him.

But maybe you picked up this book, made your way through it, and have found yourself here, close to the end, wondering about this 3G Network—<u>G</u>od the Father, <u>G</u>od the Son, <u>G</u>od the Spirit.

God the Father made you, knows more about you than you know about yourself, and loves you. In fact, He is crazy about you…but we are all separated from Him by sin.

God the Son bridged the gap, taking the punishment, the condemning, that we deserved. In paying our debt He makes it possible for us to regain our relationship with Him. It's a gift—something we can't do on our own—that He gives freely to those who place their faith in Him.

God the Spirit dwells in us, reminding us of the sacrifice, drawing us closer, growing us in holiness, convicting us and preparing us for REAL living…walking with God while we're here on earth and, after that, the eternal life of the promise!

He is the One we would like to offer to you today. If you don't know the joy and wildness of His grace, He's holding out His hand. Grab hold and hang on! Today could be the start of an incredible relationship! Believe me…Now Is Fine!

They thought they had killed Him.

His blood gushed out of His pierced side.

His head hung, lifeless.

Some felt relief. A problem had been eradicated.

Some felt sorrow. What have we done?

Some felt fright. We have done a terrible thing.

Surely now we, too, will die.

But Jesus smiled tenderly, patiently, painfully at them.

He said, "I choose to die.

"You can't take my life from me.

"I give up my life for you."

Oh, Jesus, I thought I had killed You.

I thought I had done something so bad

I could never be forgiven.

I could never atone.

And You smiled tenderly, patiently, painfully at me,

And said, "I choose to die.

"I give up my life for you.

"Your sins are forgiven.

"Go, and sin no more."

Everyone was in a good mood. They were laughing in the back seats of the van instead of the usual bickering. That was when Joel started it. "Knock, knock."

Jon, our son from Romania with Auditory Processing Disorder, quickly answered, "Come in." The squeals and roars of laughter began. "Come in? Come IN? It's supposed to be 'Who's there'." Jon got very quiet, realizing that he couldn't be a part of the jokes. That he just didn't understand. The saddest part was that he doesn't understand WHY he doesn't understand.

Knock Knock
Who's there
Tank
Tank Who
You're Welcome
(lots of laughter)

Knock, Knock
Who's there
The Boston Globe. Do you get it?
No
Neither do I. I get the New York Times.

Knock Knock
Who's there
Control Freak...now YOU say control freak who

Knock Knock
Who's there
Banana
Banana Who

Knock Knock
Who's there
Banana
Banana Who

Knock Knock
Who's there
Orange
Orange Who
Orange you glad I didn't say banana

The laughter continued as I looked into the rear view mirror and saw Jon sitting there—wanting to be a part and yet unable to participate. Because of his slower processing, his brothers and sister were just moving too fast for him.

That's when I realized…Jon was right! What we thought was a wrong answer was actually the right one…the one we SHOULD be saying, and saying boldly.

"Behold! I stand at the door and knock. If anyone hears my voice and opens the door, I will come in and eat with him, and he with Me" (Rev. 3:20 NIV).

Knock Knock
Come In.
Oh, Lord Jesus - - - *Come In!*
Now Is Fine.

What a joy it has been to watch Perry follow the Lord's leadership as he grew into the man of integrity that he is today. Perry was five years old when our family moved to the Navajo reservation to become North American missionaries. After graduation from Wayland Baptist University he married his best friend Kelley. He often adds that after more than 23 years, she is still his best friend! (She's my friend, too!) They were involved in a homeless ministry in New York City before moving to New Orleans where he attended seminary. Since 1993 his ministry has been as hospital chaplain, first in two hospitals in Nebraska and now at East Texas Medical Center in Tyler, Texas. Perry and Kelley have five children, born in three different states and two foreign countries. You will meet them in the book. What a joy and blessing it has been to work with Perry on this book. We are honored to share a part of ourselves with you.

How do you describe your mom…and still make sure you'll get invited to Thanksgiving dinner!? Most people would say she and my father Dalton are retired missionaries whose ministry included work with the Navajo Indians. Some would say she was a design editor for national Woman's Missionary Union, and Missions Mobilization Team leader for the Baptist Convention of New Mexico. Still others might point out that she has published over 600 articles, still writes adult Bible study curriculum, and has published nine books—the latest titled *Supermom Has Left the Building: Being a Proverbs 31 Woman in the 21st Century*. But my two sisters, Rhonda and Nita, and I would say we can't remember a time when her piano music didn't fill the house. And the 10 grandchildren and 3 great-grandchildren we've given my parents would say they love to visit Naana… because there is always laughter.

LaVergne, TN USA
21 October 2010
201764LV00005B/1/P